Beneath the Scar

A Story of
Resilience

Deuntay Diggs

Table of Contents

Acknowledgements

This project has been one of the hardest endeavours in my life. In the beginning, putting my life experiences on paper sounded like a great idea, an easy way to reach people and encourage them through their plights. I would soon learn that writing this book would be an emotional roller coaster, with me begging to get off the ride at times. It is one thing to have lived through this trauma, but it is a unique endeavour to relive the experiences by writing and then reading it.

I could not have completed this project without the support of my team. Each person listed below not only fulfilled the specific role listed, but in my times of doubt and fear, they encouraged me. They pushed me to remain focused on the goal of helping others, to remove pride, and to be the change I want to see in the world. I thank each of them from the bottom of my heart for believing in me.

Writing Consultant: Lorisa N. Griffith

Illustrator: Benjamin C. Monroe,

Foreword: Dylan T. Aubrecht

Photographer: Images Male

Editors: Benjamin M. Diggs

Sarah A. Martin

Amanda J. Vicinanzo

Carolanne M. Whiteside

Foreword

I first met Deuntay Diggs during a Sheriff's Office tour in early 2016. Deuntay was the First Sergeant for the Juvenile Services unit of the Stafford County Sheriff's Office. Fast forward several months later, and Deuntay and I are working side by side in the world of Law Enforcement.

After reading this book, one would've never guessed Deuntay would be where he is today. *Beneath the Scar* is a gritty, honest, first person tale about the life of Deuntay Diggs. In this book, you will join Deuntay on his journey from a small Eastern Shore kid all the way to a VMI graduate and United States Army Soldier.

The story in between though is what sets the stage in this tale of resilience. Deuntay brings the reader right into the plot with brutal truths: the abuses suffered as a child, struggling relationships with his family members, as well as coping with personal beliefs such as faith, love and sexuality.

A no-holds-barred tale, *Beneath the Scar* takes you head-on into a nightmare before making a sharp turn into the American Dream.

Dylan T. Aubrecht

Prologue

We are many, and many we are: the downtrodden, the forgotten, the battered, and abused. We have taken the worst that life has thrown at us and somehow managed to break the cycle. If one person is encouraged to dream big and go for it by reading this; realizing that even in failure there are valuable lessons learned, my intent has been accomplished.

To fully live, you must be able to forgive. Out of respect, some names, locations, and details have been altered to protect persons from scrutiny. This is not a story of revenge, but a look at life through my eyes, for time allows growth and the opportunity to heal.

I have been forged by fire and have come out with many scars. I refuse to cover my scars with makeup, or plastic surgery, for my scars make me unique.

I lay in my bed patiently waiting for everyone to fall asleep. There were ten of us staying in a four-bedroom house at the time. There was always someone up and moving around whether it was to grab water, sneak out, or use the bathroom. As the night dragged on, there was an eerie silence. Finally, everyone had gone to bed. This was the moment; this was the chance I had been waiting for.

I sat up and got out of bed as quietly as possible. I didn't want to wake my brothers. I held my breath and tiptoed past my mother's bedroom, while praying no one would catch me. The house was dark, as I slowly made my way to the kitchen with only the moonlight shining through the windows as my guide. We'd stayed here long enough that I knew where to place each step, so that I didn't make a sound.

I got to the bathroom, which was merely a couple of feet away, but it seemed like I had traveled a football field in length. I paused by the bathroom and listened, for this was my last escape route before I made a dash for it. I had reached the point of no return.

As I crossed the kitchen, my pace quickened and yet my legs felt like lead. I hurried toward a drawer near the refrigerator, quietly pulling it open and grabbing a butcher knife. Without looking around and almost at a full sprint, I sped back to my room. Once safely inside, I cautiously closed the door behind me. Suddenly, I felt like I was going to pass out--at some point during this ordeal I had stopped breathing. My heart was pounding and my breathing heavy, but as I stood just on the other side of the door, I felt a strong sense of accomplishment. Again, led by the moonlight, I stuck the knife between my mattress and the box springs. I paused for a moment and I watched as my brothers slept.

Chapter One

In the Beginning

My mother Lenora Waters was 22 years old and pregnant when she returned home to Pocomoke City, Maryland. I was her first born, and the first born in the extended family, weighing 5 pounds 1.5 ounces and measuring 19 inches. I look back at pictures during this time and I have no memories of my earliest moments in life; however, it appeared that I was surrounded by family and loved.

I was two years old when my mother had my middle brother, Tre' Quan, whose father she married, and nine years old when she had my youngest brother, Jaidyn. My mother was the oldest of four siblings, having one sister and two brothers. My grandfather was a pastor, and my grandmother played piano in the church.

As I grew up, I would hear my mother talk about being the black sheep of the family and how she felt like she was being judged. I noticed that my mother would change the way she spoke and acted when we were around the extended family, and this would annoy me.

Throughout my childhood, when things got rough, my grandparents' home was always open to us. To me, it seemed a little hypocritical that my mother felt the way she did, but I dared not question her.

My grandparents, who lived in Unionville, MD, had a two-story house that seemed like a mansion. There were four bedrooms upstairs and a bathroom. Downstairs there was a kitchen, a sitting room with a piano, a dining room, and a den. Later, as an adult, I would sometimes close my eyes and think about this place--my utopia. I can still see and feel the smiles, warmth, laughter, love and safety that emanated from their home.

2

My mother didn't like living with her parents, which isn't abnormal; but the truth is she had difficulty hiding her drug and alcohol abuse in my grandparents' home. She had to cut back, and she could only go for so long before it was time to move on. In some sense, it felt like my mother was always looking for a way back to freedom.

Some of the fondest moments of my childhood took place in Unionville and Pocomoke City. Those days included long hours spent playing childhood games such as red light-green light, hopscotch, Simon Says and hide-and-seek with my cousins and neighbors.

While at my grandparents' home, there was no fear and no worries about having the bare essentials--food and a roof over our heads. My family was like every other family.

I grew up listening to my mom, grandparents, aunt, and uncles sing, and at a young age, I tried to imitate them. One Saturday I got up in church and began to sing a solo. The congregation, in response to my singing, either covered their faces because I was singing off key or tried to sing with me, louder than me, so they could cover up my voice. I felt a little embarrassed, but I vowed to keep working on it. I idolized my grandfather, and I wanted to be just like him. I wanted to sing and dress like him and, most of all, I wanted to follow in his footsteps and become a preacher.

I also wanted to learn how to play the piano like my grandmother. I would often ask her to teach me, but she would say, "I'm not good enough to teach anyone." I never believed her. My grandmother could make a piano sing, and she had a presence that was calm and reassuring. She was the glue that held the family together and the voice of reason in moments of chaos. She also didn't take any foolishness, and could put anyone in their place with just a look.

All good things eventually come to an end. Our mom, Tre' Quan and I would leave my grandparents' house and strike out on our own. As I got older, I dreaded leaving the comfort of my grandparents' home. Life became a constant roller coaster with ups and downs, but mostly downs. Our mother married Tre' Quan's father. I don't remember the wedding or if there even was one. But I remember the days that followed, and the horror that enveloped our home as my brother's father beat our mother.

There were times that I saw her being dragged around, her fingernails gripping the floorboards and carpet as she flailed and attempted to guard herself from the vicious slaps, punches and kicks. She was small in stature, and her husband towered over her. In spite of this, she always fought back.

One evening, while standing in the living room of the apartment we stayed in, I watched as our mom was thrown through a window. Her body met the ground with a loud thud, but she sprang back up and kept fighting.

I vividly remember sitting next to her on the couch and picking the glass out of her arms as I tried to blink back tears at the sight of blood all over her face. As I cried, she looked at me and said, "Baby, Momma is alright." Even though she wouldn't admit it, I knew she was in pain.

I felt so helpless during these fights. As the oldest, I felt the need to defend my mother, but there wasn't much I could do.

Sometimes, my mother had to get the last word in during an argument, which would set her husband off. I often wished she'd just let it go, but that was not in her nature. No matter how bad the beating was, she made sure she got the last word, and she made sure he understood that she wasn't afraid of him. In my eyes, my mother was a superhero. She was unstoppable.

There were times when she was being beaten and I would get beaten trying to jump in and protect her. When I became involved, she fought even harder, like a mother bear defending her cub, even if she couldn't win. In the aftermath, my brother and I would tiptoe around the shards of shattered glass spread across the floor while maneuvering around toppled furniture and broken dishes.

Even though I envied Tre' Quan for having his father around, the jealousy was obscured by the domestic abuse. This trauma forged a special bond between him and me. Oftentimes, I would grab Tre' Quan when the fighting started, and we would escape into a different room where I would hold him tightly and tell him everything was going to be alright. Sometimes we'd cry as we listened to the yelling and the harsh sounds of various items in the household breaking. Sometimes I would leave him and go check on our mom to make sure she was okay.

I remember one time I left Tre' Quan in the bathroom when we stayed on Bonneville Avenue in Pocomoke City, MD. I found his father choking our mother on the floor near the kitchen. I will never forget the sight of my mother and the expression on her face as she clawed at him and fought for air.

Without a moment's hesitation, I grabbed a paddle that was lying on the floor that was used to beat me and my brother. I ran towards him, closed my eyes and swung as hard as I could. The paddle hit his head hard. As I turned to run, he reached out and grabbed my leg. I fell and immediately began to kick to break his grasp. One hand held me, and the other hand cradled his head. My mother, who was coughing and fighting to catch her breath, slid out from under him.

As he started to hit me, my mother grabbed a frying pan and started swinging. He let me go, and I ran back to the bathroom. I don't know how the fight ended, but eventually our mom came to the bathroom and got us, and he was gone.

Sometimes during these fights, I wanted to call the police, but I knew it would not go over well. My mother wanted to handle her own issues her way without outside interference. She would say things like, "Call the police and I'll fuck them up too." She was a little firecracker and not to be played with.

Eventually, our mother separated from my brother's father, but the memories of when and why escapes me. I just know I felt a sense of relief when he stopped coming around.

A Small Detour

Of course, not all memories of my childhood were bad. One of the card games my mother and her friends and family would play was Spades. I used to love to see her get excited and slam the card down on the table. During one of these games, one of mom's cousins gave me a two-bill and told me to split it with Tre' Quan. I ripped the bill in half and gave it to my brother as I had been told to do. The room erupted in laughter, and neither of us understood what was so funny to the adults.

Silence

In those days, home to me was wherever I laid my head on any given night. Regardless of where we lived, however, my mother would say, "What happens in this house stays in this house."

My mother made sure that Tre' Quan and I knew we were not to talk to our grandparents or anyone else about whatever issues we were having or had experienced. Oftentimes, my brother and I were left with the impression that if child protective services were contacted, they would come and take us away. To avoid this, we learned at a young age to lie, act, and be deceitful. Some would call it street smarts, but I see these things as ingredients in the recipe for failure. Tre' Quan and I were on a path to becoming just another statistic, well before we could make our own choices in life.

My brother and I lived in government-assisted living surrounded by people that we considered family. Labels were given like "cousin," "aunt," and "uncle," but often these people were just friends and not blood relatives.

One afternoon my mother left our apartment to go to my aunt's (no blood relation) house. It was a beautiful day. The sky was blue with little to no clouds and a light breeze. Tre' Quan and I, along with the kids in the neighborhood, were playing and running in and out of the house. I can still hear my mother's voice as she said, "Come through that door again and I'm going to break your back." We ran out of the house laughing, but knowing my mother wasn't playing.

As I sat on the electrical box that was in front of our apartment building with other kids from the neighborhood, our mom walked out of the building and said, "I'll be back. Behave yourselves." And off she walked.

After a while a new game of tag started up and we all ran in and out of the apartment building, around the cars and in the junkyard behind the building. Since mom was gone, the house was fair game as well.

When you stepped into our apartment, you were in the living room. Immediately to the right was the dining area, which was across from the kitchen. Further down the hall was the bathroom, and past the bathroom were two bedrooms, one on each side of the hall. My mother was so proud to be in this apartment and would often say, "This shit may not be much, but it's mine."

At one point, I was tagged "it," and I began chasing my cousin (no blood relation) Theodore because he was the closest to me. As we ran from behind the buildings through the alley, I came within arm's reach of tagging him, but every time I got close enough, he would speed up just a little faster. We continued down the alley, around a car, and back into the apartment. I thought to myself, "He's trapped, I got him." I ran into the living room behind him and, finally, I tagged him. He then immediately tagged me back and shouted "it" and ran to the bedroom I shared with my brother.

When I got to the bedroom Theodore was just standing there. He said, "I don't want to play that game anymore," so I looked at him and wondered what game we would play.

As he stood there he motioned for me to come over to him. As I did so, he pushed me down on the floor. When I rolled over to get up and ask him why he pushed me, he pulled his penis out and asked me to put it in my mouth. When I refused he grabbed my head and forced me to do it over and over again. Finally, he let go of my head and ran out of the bedroom.

I had a nasty salty taste in my mouth, so I started spitting as I ran to the bathroom with my tongue out and began rinsing my mouth out in the sink. I didn't understand what had just happened, but something inside me told me it was wrong. After I came out of the bathroom, Theodore wanted to continue to play tag; however, I didn't want to play anymore, so he ran outside. Before he left, he told me not to tell, and I had to pinky promise that I wouldn't. He was 14 years of age, and I was six years old.

As I sat on the couch, I watched the door and couldn't wait for my mother to return. When the apartment door opened, and my mother walked in, I felt a sense of relief; I immediately wanted to tell her what had happened. I wondered if I should tell her, and for a split second, I paused, then I let it all out.

My mother was known for having a quick temper and known for being outspoken. She never held back her emotions. As I told her what happened, I watched her body language for cues. She was emotionless and quiet. I had never witnessed this before. I was confused. Like smoke, my mother vanished into thin air. Without saying a word, she had left me alone standing in front of the door.

My mother returned a short while later with Lisa, Theodore's mother, and asked me to tell her what had happened. I was afraid because I felt like I had done something wrong. I didn't understand what was going on. I wasn't supposed to tell, and I had broken the pinky swear. I also could tell by both of their body language that they were worked up, tense, and angry.

As I told Lisa what had happened, she began pacing back and forth. She apologized to me and my mother and took off out the door. I could hear her through the front window as she yelled, "Theodore! Theodore, bring your motherfucking ass! Theodore!" When he came to her, she grabbed him by the back of his neck, brought him into the apartment and made him sit down in front of me.

My mother was pacing the floor at this point. Lisa had a cigarette hanging out of her mouth. I kept looking at the ash, as over half of the cigarette had burned up, but the ash was still there. She said to her son out of one side of her mouth, "What did you do to this boy?"

Theodore looked at his mom, and before he could say anything, she hit him in the chest, which knocked the wind out of him. She started beating him. As I sat there watching this, I shrank back on the couch. All I knew was that because I told on him, he was being beaten. My aunt encouraged my mother to join in, and they punched, kicked and slapped him. Lisa then dragged Theodore out of the house and into the front yard where they both continued to beat him.

I just sat on the couch and cried. I got up from the couch, briefly, looked out of the window and saw what was happening. Then, I went back to the couch, curled up into a ball, and cried. I was upset and crying because I had been beaten like that before. I felt like everything was my fault. I also realized that what he had done to me was bad to be punished for it in this way.

After it was all done, no one spoke of it again. My mom came back in and grabbed her alcohol. Theodore and Lisa left, and that was it. There was no conversation to explain what had just occurred. I took a bath and went to bed. The next day I woke up and life went on.

Months later mom took Tre' Quan and I to Lisa's house for a barbeque. As I entered the house I wondered how Theodore was going to respond to seeing me. I was shocked because it seemed like he had forgotten about what had happened. It seemed like everyone had forgotten except me.

The party started with a barbeque outside, but as night approached, everything was moved indoors. Being a true momma's boy, I led some of the kids into the kitchen where the adults were. As I walked through the door, I saw Lisa snorting what I thought was baby powder through her nose, while holding one nostril. My mom then yelled at us to get out of the kitchen and go play.

I didn't want to play. I wanted to be with my mom. I made sure throughout our time there that I kept a close eye on my brother, and I made sure we stayed with the group of kids. Something at the subconscious level was telling me to be careful even though things appeared to be normal.

I didn't want to play in the house, but it was either go play or get beaten for not doing as I was told. As I turned to walk out of the kitchen, I paused for a split second, and I thought to myself, *why is Lisa sniffing baby powder? Gross.*

When the door closed behind me, all the kids ran through the house and up the stairs. I reluctantly followed, but minutes later my concerns were alleviated as we all played in a big group in one of the rooms. We were turning off the lights and pretending to be ghosts.

Then we switched the game to hide and seek. My focus became finding the best spots to hide, and no one found me the first couple of rounds. As everyone scattered, I chose to hide under the bed in Lisa's room. I smiled ear to ear because I had the best hiding spot. Surely, I was not going to be found. I heard the footsteps coming up the stairs, and I heard Theodore say, "ready or not, here I come," and then I heard his steps coming down the hallway. It's almost as if he had a tracking device on me as he drew near. The door creaked open, and he dropped to the floor and said, "Found ya."

As I crawled out from under the bed, I tried to walk out of the room. Theodore then stepped in front of the door and closed it behind him. I immediately felt paralyzed by fear, and I couldn't move, I couldn't speak, and I couldn't scream. My mind was telling me to do something, but my body wouldn't respond. I knew I was at his mercy, but I wondered what exactly he was going to do to me this time. I could see the anger in his face; my instincts told me to get out.

He got close to me, then punched me in my chest knocking the air out of me and then began choking me. As I tried to put up a fight, he took me down to the floor and pinned me there. I tried to scream, but nothing was coming out. I pushed, pulled and kicked but it wasn't enough to make him stop. He undid my pants and just laid on top of me. It was almost as if the more I fought back, the more excited he got.

I started praying to God for someone to walk in and save me. I was on my stomach, and out of nowhere I felt an intense pain. I felt like I was going to pass out. I lay there for what felt like hours and became numb. As I lay there, it was almost as though I had left my body, and I was looking down and watching what was happening to me. Finally, he stopped, got up and walked out of the room.

Exhausted, I lay in the spot where he left me. Suddenly, I had the urge to have a bowel movement. I wanted to get to my mom, but I knew I wasn't going to make it; so, I went into the bathroom, locked the door, and I sat on the toilet in pain. As I sat on the toilet, I tried to go, but nothing happened. I stood up and looked, and there wasn't much in the toilet. I reached for the toilet paper and wiped, and I noticed blood running down the back and inside of my thighs. At the sight of blood, I started to lose control of my emotions and began to cry inconsolably.

Theodore broke into the bathroom, defeating the lock as if it was nothing. As he walked in, he grabbed me by the throat again. He told me that if I told anyone, he would kill me. Something in the way he looked at me and the way he said it led me to believe he really meant it.

At six years old, that moment came to define me in ways I would have never imagined. When he left, I cleaned up. I realized there was no one to protect me and that I had to learn to protect myself. I was robbed of my childhood in that moment. I knew my mother loved me. That was never a question. I just didn't think she had the skills to deal with everything that was going on when I was a child.

I had told her about the first time I was sexually abused, but I knew that due to the drug and alcohol abuse, she wasn't always going to be there to protect me. I made a choice to try to survive by not saying anything. I became hypersensitive of my actions because I was afraid someone would find out. I learned to control my emotions, and I learned to become a chameleon in order to blend in. I knew that if I said anything, eventually Theodore would be able to get to me. Oftentimes I wondered what my mother would have done had she known.

I wandered around the house and fell asleep on the floor in a corner in one of the bedrooms on the second floor. When I woke up the next morning, I kept thinking about what had happened; I thought about it repeatedly as I lay there.

The other kids in the house were up and running around about the same time that I woke up. Most of them were upset because they had been in there hiding places for so long the night before that they had fallen asleep. When I saw Theodore for the first time, he acted as if nothing had happened. At this moment I realized he had concealed his feelings and emotions and had taken acting lessons as well. It was almost like I had had a bad dream, but the soreness I felt reminded me it wasn't so.

As time went on, I tried to stay closer to my mother to prevent it from happening again. When the adults would hang out, they always shooed the kids away and told us to go play. My mother didn't know that I tried to stay close to her to protect myself.

When we lost our apartment and ended up moving in with Theodore and his family, the sexual abuse happened more and more. As I grew older, I would fight or do everything I could to avoid him because I was determined that I wasn't going to keep being hurt. After a while, Theodore got tired of fighting, so he told me, "if you don't do it, your brother will."

I knew then, at approximately eight years old, that I had to protect Tre' Quan at all costs. There was nothing I wouldn't do to ensure that he was okay. There wasn't even a pause or deliberation as I decided what needed to be done.

There were times when Tre' Quan would be a few feet away from me while the molestation was occurring, and I assumed that he was asleep. Over time escaping my body in those moments and being somewhere else -on a beach, singing on a stage, or on my private airplane -made all the difference. I lived out fantasies in my head, longing for someone to protect me, for someone to take me away from what was going on. I prayed, but it seemed like God couldn't hear me. Hindsight being 20/20, God answered my prayers, just not the way I expected him to.

Lisa and my mother were close friends, but they would get into arguments and my mom would say to Tre' Quan and me, "Pack your shit up, we getting out of this raggedy motherfucker." The breaks in staying with Lisa gave me time to heal both physically and mentally. I was glad to leave each time even though most of the time we didn't have anywhere to go.

The first couple of times we returned, I felt sick knowing what was going to happen, but eventually even those emotions would fade. There was no question of why me; it was just life as I knew it.

A Random Act of Kindness

As we moved from place to place, staying with friends and cousins in the area, we'd eventually wear out our welcome. The last time we stayed with Lisa, like every time before, we packed up what little bit we had and left. This time we left in the middle of the winter night during a snow storm. My mother, brother, and I walked down 4th Street in Pocomoke City, MD towards the train tracks.

As we approached Mitchell's Market a car pulled over, and a woman got out and asked my mother if we needed anything. My mother said, "No," as we continued to walk. The woman walked back to her car, opened the backdoor, took the coats off her children, and gave one to me and one to my brother. She gave me the Dallas Cowboys jacket, and Tre' Quan got the Baltimore Ravens jacket.

These were the first Starter brand name jackets that we ever owned. This act of kindness is something I will never forget; it also made me a Cowboys fan for life. I felt so upset towards our mom for not allowing this lady to help us. My brother and I were exhausted and cold. I still hear my mother's voice as she told us, "We almost there." All too often my mother's pride and stubbornness got in the way.

Discipline

As we made it to her friend's house off Clementine St., we walked in, and I saw sheets and blankets hung in front of all the entrances into the living room. There was a kerosene heater in the middle of the room and a pot on top of the heater with water in it.

Tre' Quan and I were so relieved. We went and sat as close as we could to the heater. We were given food and put to bed in the living room on a pullout sofa bed. The next morning when we woke up, I didn't want to move because it was so cold; the kerosene heater had gone out during the night while we slept.

The one thing I hated about the new home was that there was no toilet. That meant no matter how cold it was, if I had to use the bathroom, I had to go outside to an outhouse. One morning I had to pee so badly, but I didn't want to get up, so I laid there and peed in the bed. The whipping that I got for doing it ensured from that point on I would brave the cold. Our mother's favorite saying was "I brought you into this world and I can take you out." In that moment I believe she tried.

Our mother was tough on me when it came to punishment. One time she was eating chicken tenders and fries, and without asking, I reached to grab a fry. Within the blink of an eye I felt a sharp pain between my pinky and ring finger on my right hand. My mother had stabbed me with her fork. I had a scar there for a long time, and in that moment, I learned rather quickly not to put my hands on people's plates.

Rolling your eyes and sucking through your teeth could almost get you killed when I was growing up. On one occasion I told my mother after she had beaten me that I was going to call the cops on her. She replied, "If you want to call 9-1-1, go ahead. Let social services take you." I picked up the phone, she struck me across my hand, and I dropped the phone. It took me a second to catch my breath, so the cry could come out. She then said, "Go lay your ass down, and stop crying before I give you a reason to cry."

Another time I was standing on the edge of the bathtub, and my mother told me a couple of times to get down, I sucked through my teeth and rolled my eyes, and in the next second I thought I saw heaven. My mother yanked my leg, and I fell, hitting my head on the tub faucet. One of her friends came in, and I can remember the shock on her face when she saw the blood everywhere. She told my mom to call for an ambulance, and my mom said, "He'll be alright." She refused to call an ambulance; she said, "They're not going to lock my black ass up."

She looked at me, looked away, and then looked back a second time and said, "Stop that damn crying before I give you something to cry about." I lay there, and thought I was going to die. Eventually my head was wrapped with a towel, and I was sent to bed.

One day in school I decided to be the funny kid, and I was disrespectful to a teacher. My mom was called about it. By the time I got home from school, I had forgotten about what I had done. I walked into the house, and my mom said, "Go take a shower. You're in the house for the night since you don't know how to act." In my mind I thought, *That's it? I don't mind staying in the house.*

I got into the shower and started singing; I was so into my song that I didn't hear my mother come into the bathroom. She snatched the curtain back and I felt a stinging and burning sensation. I realized that my mother was beating me with an extension cord. I hit notes higher than Patti in that moment.

I fell out of the shower wrapped up in the shower curtain. I ran through the house as she chased me. I slid under the dining room table, but like the Incredible Hulk, my mother flipped it over and kept swinging. I can look back now as an adult and find the humor in these moments, but it's only by the grace of God that I was never seriously injured.

An Empty Shell

While in Pocomoke City, MD, I attended both elementary and middle school up to the fourth grade. School was not my primary focus as a kid. I guess most kids don't focus in school at such a young age.

I had so much going on that school was a temporary relief from the chaos and uncertainty I faced when I got home. Kids would pick on me because my clothes smelled due to the kerosene heater, my ears were big, or because my mother had bad teeth. It was what it was. When I would tell my mom what happened, she would say, "Fuck 'em." My mother exuded confidence and pride even in her darkest moments.

My teachers often filled in when my mom couldn't for activities such as Field Day. Even though I gave my teachers hell, I still respected them. A lot of the acting out I did in school was to distract from the pain I was feeling on the inside. For me school wasn't a place to learn; it was a place to eat and to sleep.

Some teachers would get annoyed with me because I slept in class, not realizing that often times, depending on where we lived, I wasn't sleeping at home. I went through an emotional rollercoaster of pain, anguish, and despair as a child. Teachers that would smile or give me a hug would lift my spirits and do more for me in those moments than a scolding or referral could have ever done.

I was the class clown because I thought it made me cool and it took my mind off the issues in my life. Teachers would initially call my mom when I acted out. Though they didn't know the extent of my punishment when I got home, eventually they stopped calling her. I believe that deep down inside they knew something was not right. Maybe it was because they saw welts or bruises on my arms and legs.

Social services were called a couple of times, but they never did much. My mom knew what to do and say to get around the system. She was evasive and knew how to talk to them. She was good at throwing people off. She could tell you a lie, and you'd know it was a lie, but she could sell it to you and make you believe it was the truth. She was good at forcing her idea of reality or perspective onto others.

My extended family knew things were not good; but, because of the way my mother could present, they never knew how bad things really were. My childhood was spent trying to survive and mask the pain, guilt, and anxiety. I worked hard at it and was successful at projecting the image that everything was okay, all the while dying on the inside.

Matthew 6:25

Sometimes my brother and I would get to participate in fun activities like camping or church events with extended family. These small reprieves just gave me a glimpse of how life was supposed to be, and showed me how tumultuous my life really was.

Many of my fond memories of moments as a child revolved around eating. One time during the summer our mother took my brother and me to the river to go crabbing. She taught us how to put the chicken on a string, and put it into the water and let it sink. After waiting for a while, I'd pull up the string and take the crab net, going under gently, and catch crabs. Then our mother would put some beer and Old Bay in a pot with the crabs and cook them.

One of my favorite meals that our mother made was chicken and dumplings. I would sit in the kitchen, watch her, and then imitate her actions. She would give me a look and bust out laughing.

I also loved going to church as a child. When it came time for communion, I would think to myself, *fill me up lord,* as I tried to sneak extra grape juice and wafers. I also couldn't wait for potluck after service, though it almost never seemed like there was enough food.

<u>One More Can't Hurt</u>

At nine years old -as if life wasn't already hard enough- my mother had my youngest brother, Jaidyn. As mom walked across the kitchen floor, she tripped on an extension cord in the kitchen, which sent her into labor. I didn't understand what was really going on at the time. All I knew was that strangers came in, put our mother on a bed with wheels, and took her away.

As I cried and attempted to run after the ambulance, I was stopped by one of her friends who told me that everything was going to be okay.

A few days later mom showed up with this little thing that wouldn't stop crying and seemed to get all her attention. I didn't want him, and I didn't like him. I was okay with sharing my mother with Tre' Quan, but not anyone else. That was until I got to hold my baby brother for the first time.

I sat on the couch, with Tre' Quan beside me, and our mother placed Jaidyn in my arms. As I stared at him and he looked around the room, my opinion changed, and in that moment, I came to terms with having another brother.

As a child I was led by lessons I learned in church. I attended Seventh-Day Adventist and sometimes Pentecostal denominations. Church was a place where I felt safe; it was my refuge. During the most horrific times in my childhood, it was faith that got me through.

As my brothers and I got older, we would find stable places to live for a short period of time. My mother had several boyfriends over the years, and it seemed like it would never fail that almost all these men at some point would beat her.

Once we lived in Hallwood, VA with one of her boyfriend's, Mike, who ran an assisted living house for adults. As the fighting between the two escalated, Mike eventually asked mom to move out. He did, however, offer to rent her a trailer on the property. Mom was told to pick any trailer on the property that was vacant, and we could live there. So, she and I walked down Shorty Dr. As we got to the back of the property, both of our eyes lit up and together we chose our new home.

I was so excited, but as we got the key and gained access to the trailer, we saw that the inside was trashed. The outside looked amazing, but the inside had rotten food, cobwebs, clothes piled high, roaches, and rodents. Me, Tre' Quan and our mother all cleaned together, and in about three days we had the trailer looking amazing.

About a month later mom was told that Mike's brother was getting out of jail and that he wanted his trailer back. Well, of course, his trailer was the one we had spent so much time on and were living in. I was furious, but my mother told me to stay out of grown folks' business. We ended up choosing another trailer right behind the assisted living house. This was the next best one on the property, but it had lots of issues that needed to be fixed.

The porch was falling apart, the windows didn't have a good seal, the floor was weak, there was no door on the bathroom, and half of the cabinets in the kitchen were missing doors. Still, we had a home, and by this point in life I had learned to appreciate the little things. The first day we stayed in the new trailer was horrible. It was raining, and it was cold. We didn't have any heat, nor did we have any food.

I remembered mom coming home with a hair net and black boots from time to time. She worked at a chicken plant during this time and had to leave for work. As she left my brothers and me, I made a pile in the middle of the living room floor with blankets. Shivering cold and hungry, we remained there until our mom got back home.

About a week later we got the lights turned on and a kerosene heater appeared. I hated the damn heater so badly because of the strong odor, but I loved it for the warmth it provided. At this point I noticed that even when we didn't have food, my mother always had alcohol. This began to annoy me, but I dared not say anything about it, for a coma or possibly death would surely follow.

A Familiar Pain

One of the selling points about continuing to live in Hallwood was my mother's friend Erica, whom she worked with. Erica, her husband Charles, and their two daughters rented a trailer on the property as well. Their trailer was red but wasn't in the best of shape either.

There was something about everyone struggling to survive that made life so much more bearable in those days. As things got better, Erica and Charles and their daughters would hang out in our trailer and play Spades. I didn't really have a father figure in my life, so I looked up to Charles, especially since he was in the military.

Given all the trauma I had experienced, at this point in my life I was good at reading people. I was in tune at looking for micro expressions that others would miss. As time went on I knew I needed to stay away from Charles. The admiration I had for him dissipated, and I was left feeling on edge and anxious when he was around.

As days turned to weeks and weeks to months he didn't do anything inappropriate at first; however, I didn't second guess my instincts. I stayed alert, and I kept a watchful eye on my siblings. I had learned my lesson the first time.

One evening while the women played cards, Charles, my brothers and I wrestled in the living room. Without warning he scooped me up and said to my brothers I'm taking him with me. I tried to get down, but he held onto me tight. My brothers were laughing and swinging for me. We walked past the kitchen table with my brothers following and walked down the hall. I screamed, "Put me down!" He put his hand over my mouth to muffle my voice. As we got to the first room I grabbed onto the door jam. With ease he pulled me into the room releasing my grip. My brothers were laughing, but I was panic stricken.

As we wrestled in the dark he grabbed my buttocks a couple of times and stuck his hands down the front of my pants touching my penis. He then said, "I didn't mean to do that," and he let me go.

As time went on he eventually was left to babysit us while his wife and my mom went out on the town. I told my mom that I could take care of my brothers, and that we didn't need a babysitter, but she refused to listen. Why wouldn't she just listen? I never questioned anything that life threw at me, but all I wanted was for my mother to see me and hear me.

The first night, he was left to watch his daughters, my brothers and me. It was getting late, and so we were all put to bed. His daughters went into their room, and Jaidyn slept on the couch, while Tre' Quan and I lay on the floor in a blanket.

I woke up to Charles standing over me. I laid there for a while pretending that I was sleeping hoping he would go away. As he knelt beside me I felt like my heart was going to beat out of my chest. He then tapped me on the shoulder a couple of times and I turned over on my side facing Tre' Quan, at which point Charles grabbed my shoulder and started shaking me.

I sat up and started wiping my eyes as if I was confused about what was going on. Charles told me to get up and go lay in the bed where it was more comfortable. I already knew where this was going to go, but I got up and walked into his room and crawled onto the bed. He walked in behind me and shut the door.

He then lay on the bed. He was wearing sweatpants with a military logo on them and a green shirt with holes. He removed his shirt and lay on the bed next to me. I wasn't afraid; at this point I was desensitized. He motioned for me to come closer and had me lay my head on his chest. He then grabbed my left hand and placed it on his penis which was hard. He asked, "Do you like that?" I didn't respond. He told me to "kiss it." As he pulled his pants down there was a foul smell. I backed away at which point he pushed my head toward his penis with his left arm.

As he rubbed his penis on my lips and face I tried to hold my breath. "Open your mouth and lick it," he said. Eventually he ejaculated in my mouth and I spit his semen out. He then slapped me in the mouth and said, "You need to swallow it." Charles then told me to go lay down.

I walked out of his bedroom and lay back in my spot on the floor. I lay there thinking, *is this how life was going to be?* I had escaped one monster only to find another. I began questioning what was wrong with me.

The next day when I woke up, Charles was up fixing breakfast. His daughters came out of their room and we were told to come into the kitchen and grab food. Erica was in her nightgown with no bra on standing by Charles. Her breasts were hanging, and I thought to myself, *gross put a bra on.* I looked at Erica and asked, "Where is my mom?"

She looked at me and said, "She went home. Go sit your little bad ass down!"

I replied, "Yes Ma'am." I was confused about why she was being so snappy. I sat on the floor by the couch with my food, but I didn't eat. Erica walked over to me and grabbed the plate and said, "You're not going to waste my motherfucking food. Go home."

As I got up, walked to the door and put on my shoes, I looked back for my brothers. She walked over at a quick pace and grabbed my arm and yanked me outside. Once outside Erica said, "I should tell your momma that you came on to my husband last night. Are you a sissy?"

I said, "No Ma'am."

She said, "I don't want any faggots around my husband. If you ever come on to my husband again I'm going to beat your sissy ass." As she walked into the house and closed the door I heard her say, "little faggot liar."

At that moment I ran from the porch and down Shorty Dr. to the back of the property. I got to the woods and I ran, then I got to the fields and I ran until I couldn't run anymore. I cried, and snot ran out of my nose. In my head I thought, *No one will ever believe me. There's nothing I can do but run away.* So, I ran until I fell from exhaustion. I lay there angry as I asked myself why he had lied about me.

I then had a moment of clarity, and I realized that I couldn't run away because no one would protect my brothers. I got up and made my way back home, and it was if I had never left. My mom was drinking her alcohol in the living room and my brothers were playing.

Because of the first ordeal, when mom would leave, I would cry and tell her not to go; she would tell me to "man up" or "grow up" because she needed to have fun and she was tired of dealing with us "bad ass kids." She had a lot on her plate dealing with us and trying to provide for us. It was what it was.

Eventually, Charles got more and more comfortable with molesting me. It was like clockwork, like a routine. He'd knock on my window at night. I would walk out of the front door and he would be waiting by the front porch. I would then follow him to the abandoned house to the left of his trailer where he either sodomized me or I'd perform oral sex on him.

Charles knew that he could take advantage of my mother's drunken-state as he molested me near our home. It didn't matter anymore at this point; I had lost hope. What was the use in fighting? If I didn't go at night, eventually, when left in his care, it would be much worse. I had seen flashes of his temper, and I wanted to make sure that I didn't upset him.

I learned at these moments to play the long game; nothing lasts forever. It was not the time to be emotional. I had to look at the brighter side and maintain focus on my brothers.

A Fresh Start

Eventually my mother started a new relationship, and we moved on to a new location in Horntown, VA. In this home was a blended family. My mom and we three boys were living with her boyfriend, Shawn, and his four kids and grandchild. In this house domestic abuse occurred between my mother and Shawn, but not as often as it had in the past.

As you walked up the steps and into the house, you entered a living room. If you walked straight back, you would be in the kitchen. To the left was Shawn's bedroom, the bedroom I shared with my brothers, and the bathroom. To the right were two more bedrooms. The one on the front of the house was Shawn's daughter's room, which she shared with her own daughter, and the one on the back was split between Shawn's three boys.

The family blended well even though Shawn's children were older than my brothers and I. For the most part everyone got along; I was closest with his daughter Nikki. She was rebellious and would fight with her dad. Nikki was tough and didn't care what her dad would say; she was going to do whatever she wanted with whomever she wanted.

Nikki used to sneak guys in through my bedroom. They would come through my window, sneak through the house, and into her room and then back out the way they came. Nikki knew her brothers would never stand for it, so she depended on me to keep her secret.

Onetime Shawn saw footprints on the ground behind the house, and noticed the screen was bent from being taken off. For whatever reason, I was picked as the culprit. After being questioned repeatedly about climbing out of the window at night and denying it, I was still beaten for it. I held on to the secret, and it made the bond between Nikki and I even closer.

With so many mouths to feed, food went fast in the house. Eventually a chain was put around the refrigerator to account for who was eating what. There was no just going into the kitchen and getting something to eat. You had to ask for what you wanted. One time I was so hungry that I went to Shawn's cousin's house, which was next door, and ate dog food out of a trash can where it was kept by a shed. I remember eating it and being shocked that it tasted good.

Education

Living in Horntown, VA meant we went to school on Chincoteague Island. We were considered mainlanders. Some days the entire trip, approximately forty-five minutes to school and back, was a nightmare. It meant forty-five minutes of being taunted because I was the new kid, whereas, most of the other kids had grown up together and were kin.

I attended Chincoteague Elementary and Middle School for 5th, 6th, and part of 7th grade. I hated school because I had horrible test-taking skills and it took me much longer than my peers to understand most theories and concepts.

Sitting still and trying to learn was a punishment to me. I went from one extreme to the other: either I was sleeping, or I was high energy. My mind never stopped either way, so I was constantly thinking of different things and found it hard to focus.

The one subject I was introduced to that kept me engaged was music. In music I found my voice. For so long I hadn't been able or allowed to communicate how I felt, but through playing an instrument, I could speak without saying a word. Up to this point I could smile with the best of them even though, figuratively, I felt like death on the inside.

Raising a Black Man-Child

My mother was tough on me because of the environment I was being raised in and because she was a single mother for most of my childhood. She was a fierce disciplinarian.

If I looked at her the wrong way or raised my voice, I'd get hit. She did not tolerate any disrespect. She would beat me with anything she could get her hands on, and then she'd brag about it. High heeled shoes, extension cords, lamps, pans, it didn't matter. If she could lift it, she'd hit us with it.

Being the oldest, I often got the brunt of the beatings. One day I got tired of it. She was beating me for something I said or did wrong, and she was hitting me with a belt. I grabbed the belt and she saw that as my attempt at challenging her. Because I wouldn't let go of the belt, she started punching me while screaming, "I'll kill you, motherfucker."

That beating lasted a while. She left, and I lay there for a little bit, then I got a shirt to wipe my face. I realized that my face wasn't just wet from crying, but that I was also bleeding. I walked outside to the front porch. The looks on the faces of my brothers and the neighbors outside was one of total shock. It was the first time I'd heard anyone threaten to call social services on my mother.

I had welts on my back, and arms, my lips were swollen, my eyes were swollen, and my nose was bleeding. One of the neighbors said, "Child there's nothing you could have done to deserve being beaten like that." People felt so bad for me. Their concern touched me, but the truth is, though I felt the pain, I was numb and had given up on life.

My mother never said anything to me about it, but Shawn pulled me aside later that night and told me that she regretted losing her temper with me.

The only time I ever heard of my mother saying that she regretted anything she did was that beating, and she never mentioned it to me. She never mentioned it to me because it would be considered showing weakness. I often wondered if she knew how much I loved her.

This beating sent me into a downward spiral. It was the beating that would ultimately shut out the light at the end of the tunnel. *What reason did I have to go on, who would even care if I was gone?* I felt like garbage. The only reprieve I got was when I slept, which wasn't much. As soon as my eyes opened, my thoughts were sporadic and chaotic. I was constantly stressed about utilities, food and safety. I just wanted everything to stop.

That night as I lay down and Tre' Quan checked over me and asked if I was okay, I lay there on my back tears running down my face as I repeated, "I'm fine." I decided that night that I was done. Over the weekend my bruises healed, but I was kept out of school a couple of days to ensure there weren't going to be any reports to child protective services (CPS). When I returned to school, kind words from teachers helped me cope, but spending the day in school was temporary, and I had to eventually return home.

A Chameleon

The week prior to enacting my plan was one of the best weeks of my life. No matter what anyone said, or did, it didn't matter. I had not a care in the world; I was at peace. The only frustration I had was figuring out when, where, and how I was going to commit suicide. On the seventh day, God had rested, and so would I.

I finished out school that Friday, and as I rode home on the bus, I literally couldn't hear the taunts from the other kids. I was in my own world, as I made it through Friday night and all of Saturday. I thought about things I had heard adults say. I didn't know much about suicide, but I had heard someone say that if you cut your wrist going up the train tracks and not across them, it would ensure you couldn't be brought back. I didn't have access to guns, I didn't have access to medicine, but I could get a knife.

I realized that getting a knife out of the kitchen was going to be risky, and I was going to have to wait until everyone went to bed. It seemed a small price to pay to be free of the chaos. That night as we were put to bed, I gave Mom a hug and told her I loved her. She replied, "I love you, baby," and she walked out of the room.

The waiting game had begun. As the seconds turned to minutes and the minutes to hours, I could hear everyone starting to go to bed. I started to get tired, but I was determined to complete my mission. I lay in my bed patiently waiting for everyone to fall asleep. As the night dragged on finally there was an eerie silence. Finally, everyone had gone to bed. This was the moment; this was the chance I had been waiting for.

I sat up and got out of bed as quietly as possible so that I didn't wake my brothers. I held my breath, and I tiptoed past my mother's bedroom while praying no one would catch me. The house was dark, and the moonlight shining through the kitchen was my guide. We'd stayed there long enough that I knew where to place each foot so that I didn't make a sound.

I got to the bathroom, which was merely a couple of feet away, but it seemed like I had traveled a football field. I paused by the bathroom and listened, for this was my last escape route before I made a dash for it. I had reached the point of no return. On my tiptoes I quickly walked into the kitchen, opened the drawer, grabbed a butcher knife, and quickly returned to my room.

As I entered my room and closed the door behind me, I felt like I was going to pass out; at some point during this ordeal I had stopped breathing. My heart was pounding, my breathing was heavy, and I felt a strong sense of accomplishment. I was amazed that I could feel something; I had been numb for quite some time. Again, led by the moonlight, I stuck the knife between the mattress and the box springs. I paused for a moment, and I watched my brothers sleep. Then I returned to my place in bed and fell asleep with ease.

The next day when I woke up, I felt refreshed. It had been quite some time since I had had a good night's sleep. I lay in the bed for a while looking out of the window into the woods as the sun was shining through the window. I was alone in the room as my brothers had woken up early and were off doing something; everything was quiet.

I sat up and moved to the edge of the bed and I grabbed the butcher knife. I started to rock and say to myself, "up the railroad tracks not across the railroad tracks." I took the knife out from under the mattress and put it to my wrist. I began to push down.

As I began pushing, the door behind me opened. I looked back, and I didn't see anyone there. I felt the mattress shake and Jaidyn, who was about two or three at the time, popped up onto the mattress. He crawled across the mattress and put his arms around me. Still holding onto him, I put the knife back underneath the mattress and began to cry.

The light that had not been there at the end of the tunnel began to shine brightly. I realized I had gotten lost. I had begun to focus on myself too much. I focused on my needs and my expectations of what I thought a childhood should be. I focused on all the negativity that had happened. I realized that my purpose for living was to make sure that my brothers were alright. I had to be there for them.

I promised myself as long as God gave me breath and the ability to do so, I was going to protect them. I had a new perspective and outlook on life. It wasn't the past that mattered, it was the future. Throughout my childhood I had sat in many different churches and listened to pastors who had at one point or another spoken of forgiveness. I didn't know how to, but I knew that if I was going to make it, I had to, for my sanity and for my future, forgive those who had hurt me. So, I prayed, and it was as if a weight was lifted off of my shoulders.

As had happened many times before, our mom's relationship with Shawn ended, and we were on the move again. Our next stop was Parksley, VA. While there I attended the remainder of my 7th grade year and 8th grade at Parksley Middle School. I rarely got to participate in school events, and my mother almost never came to school events. She didn't have time for that.

It was difficult for me as a kid because I'd see other children's parents volunteering or coming to have lunch with them. I didn't get to have that experience. All through school I participated in anything dealing with music. I learned rather quickly that music was my outlet.

I started out in concert band in middle school and moved on to the marching band. My band directors played a very important role throughout my childhood because they were the ones who would get me to and from practice, events and competitions.

The trombone was my instrument of choice and the first instrument that I learned how to play. I chose it because I had big lips and a trumpet mouthpiece was too small. I didn't think that the flute was the appropriate instrument to fit my personality, so I ended up in the low brass section.

At 12 years old I had lived through more than some experience in a lifetime. But something was different after my suicide attempt. I cherished each moment. I learned to accept what was and to focus on where I wanted to be. I just hoped that I would get the opportunity to graduate.

Our next home was in a trailer park named Dreamland, which was more like a nightmare in terms of living conditions. We lived in a rodent-infested, roach-infested trailer. We eventually set off foggers to clear the roaches out, but we struggled to get rid of the rodents. There were times I would lie on the couch and watch rats come up through holes in the floor. I would be scared to move, as I'd watch them run across the counter.

These country rats were as big as squirrels! These problems weren't isolated just to our trailer though; across the trailer park one of mom's close friends had a rat bite her foot while she slept in a recliner. Hearing about it and seeing the wound left me wanting to find a way to kill all rodents.

But, like many times before, we made it work. Though we struggled, I must say this was the best time in my childhood because it was just my brothers, our mom and me.

Momma's Boy

Even though I experienced a lot of trauma at a young age, my mother was still my world. As a child everything that happened to me, all of the bad experiences, never caused me to resent my mother. I don't know why that is really.

I saw her struggle, and I knew deep down inside that she wanted the best for me and my brothers. I always believed that she did the best she could. She did the best she knew how to do as a mother. There were times when her personality would light up a room as she cracked jokes and laughed. Later on in life she was often called "Madea," after Tyler Perry's character, because of the similarities. My mother would take her alcohol to church and drink it out in the parking lot.

My mother's alcohol addiction was bad; it seemed like she could stop the drugs at any time, but her alcohol addiction went on throughout my whole childhood.

There were times when she would be passed out drunk and would throw up. I would sit beside her and watch her sleep. I was concerned that she would die, so I would spend hours watching her chest rise up and down with each breath she took. She would pass out on her back, and I would wedge myself between her and the sofa and roll her over onto her side.

Though I was just a kid, these situations were common sense to me. No one told me to do it. I just somehow knew it was the right thing to do to prevent her from choking to death on her own vomit. Mom put up a facade that everything was okay; we were more alike in this than we both realized at the time. She was fiercely independent, and she wanted people to know that she was strong. Her personality often put me in situations I wasn't supposed to be in.

I wanted a clean house as a kid. My method of cleaning didn't make much sense because I had to mess everything up and then clean. I couldn't have some area that was partially dirty and only clean the part that was dirty. I loved to dance while I cleaned, and I found over time that I was great at organizing things.

One time I was cleaning the trailer and a song titled 'Jesus Is My Help' by gospel artist Hezekiah Walker came on. I went and got my mom's high-heeled shoes and I was dancing around in the kitchen. Mom walked into the trailer and started laughing. I remember that moment fondly, as mom snapped her fingers and started singing.

Mom's first priority was work, especially when she had all three of us, but drinking and partying took up a lot of her time as well. Watching my mother bounce back time after time amazed me as a child. Nothing was beneath her as far as work; she would do whatever she needed to do in order to take care of us.

When she was around her friends, she was never too proud to say if she was on food stamps or was using government assistance. She was the type of person that acted like it was what it was; take it or leave it, she didn't care. In the streets, in the community she told people how she really felt. I admired that.

Two Paths Diverge

As Tre' Quan and I grew up, we began to take different paths in life. He wanted the fast money and the gang life, but I wasn't having it. We would often fight, and he would say, "You're nnnot my dddady," with a stammer as I would try to guide him in the right direction. "You're not my daddy." He knew I struggled with not knowing my biological father, so he would bring it up to get back at me for not allowing him to do whatever he wanted to.

These types of arguments led to me asking our mom about my biological father. She would never answer. I would ask, "Who is my dad?" and she would make jokes like, "it's the mailman," or she would say that she was my father. She would rarely discuss the topic with me.

I constantly looked for my dad. I wondered if he looked like me, or if I sounded like him when I talked. Once she told me that when she revealed to my biological father that she was pregnant, he told her he was married, and he wanted her to have an abortion. In my asking about my biological father, my mother's response let me know it was an insult to even ask about him and that it was painful to her, so eventually I stopped asking.

Tre' Quan and I loved to play outside with other kids in the trailer park. We would run through the woods and hang out in a fort we built out of random materials like broken branches, pallets and tires.

Sometimes while we hung out at the fort, some of the neighborhood kids would smoke marijuana or drink alcohol that they had stolen from their parents. As time went by, I noticed that Tre' Quan was drinking and using marijuana more and more. I had only smoked marijuana once at this point, and I realized rather quickly it wasn't for me.

Tre' Quan and I stayed at one of mom's friend's trailers, and her son-in-law thought it was a good idea to get both of us and his brother-in-law high. As all four of us sat in a circle, I grabbed the blunt and inhaled wrong and burned my throat. That was it for me. Once mom's friend found out what had happened, she kept us out of sight of our mom and told mom she would keep us for a few days to give her some rest. This was so she could make sure my throat healed.

Over time Tre' Quan and I would physically fight because I would break his blunt or smash his bottle of alcohol, but I was trying to talk some sense into him. In my mind I was trying to protect him. I would come to realize later that I was pushing him further and further away. I loved our mother, but doing these things, in my mind, meant he was destined to repeat her failures and I wanted better for him.

A Wrong Turn

As I hung out in the woods and ran through the trailer park with the rest of the kids, a guy by the name of Scott eventually appeared. Scott was in his mid-20's, and he would sometimes provide alcohol for everyone that hung out at the fort. Scott was a security guard, but at first glance I thought he was a cop.

The first couple of times he came around, I instantly felt like something was wrong. I had met him before- his eyes, the expressions on his face. I was shocked that it seemed like I was the only one who knew that something was wrong.

Being in this group of kids was a little different than before because we all stuck together. The only issue is that when Tre' Quan and the rest of the kids started drinking or even smoking, I would leave. We had to be in by dark anyway and most times Scott showed up an hour or two before dark.

One evening as I walked home, Scott left the other kids and started following me. I wish I could say I was scared or shocked, but this was familiar to me. As I kept walking, he said, "Wait up," I just kept walking. As I neared the wood line, Scott said, "Let me make sure you get home safely." In my head, I was thinking, *sure, that's all you want.*

As we walked across the trailer park, Scott started asking questions about me having a girlfriend, and if I'd had sex. I just listened to him talk but didn't respond much. I could see my trailer across the field, and my focus was just getting there. It was dusk, so I wasn't worried about him doing anything out in the open, but I just wanted to get away from this creep. I made it to the trailer, and I realized that my mom wasn't home. The green Malibu Classic that my mom drove wasn't in the yard. Scott asked, "Where is your mom?"

I replied, "She's on her way home." He asked if I wanted him to stay until she got home, and I told him that my mother didn't want anyone in her trailer.

He left, and I closed the door and locked it. I turned on the kerosene heater, and I put a pot of water on top to keep moisture in the air. I sat and waited for both our mom and brothers to get home.

As it got later and later, I began to worry about Tre' Quan. He knew if mom beat him home, she was going to try and kill him, but he didn't care. He was getting more and more stubborn. So, I headed out to find him, but as I walked the loop in the trailer park, he was nowhere to be found.

I went back to the fort, frustrated and ready to fight him for making me look for him. Finally, I found him at a friend's trailer. I knocked, and a lady came to the door. I asked if Tre' Quan was there, and she said, "Hold up," and closed the door.

When he appeared at the door and stuck his head out. I told him, "Let's go. You know you're supposed to be home." He grabbed his shoes and walked out. We argued and yelled at each other the whole walk home.

Once we were back home, Tre' Quan realized that our mom still wasn't there, and he was mad at me for making him come home. Finally, mom came home with Jaidyn and all was well.

As Scott showed up more and more, eventually he got around to asking me if I ever had a blow job from a girl. I responded with, "Of course," though this wasn't the case at all. He would go on to ask me if he could give me head, and I'd respond, "No. I'm good."

As his advances kept getting denied, he would eventually get angry, and one evening he said, "You're going to do it for me." I shrugged my shoulders and I thought to myself, *let's get this over with; this is nothing new.* In my head I questioned, *what took you so long to get to the point?*

I was smart enough to see the game unfolding. Where he had won over all the other kids with the alcohol and hanging out, I knew his real intent. I countered where I could, but the reality, my reality, was that the ending was going to be the same.

As we stood between the woods and the trailer closest to the trail we used to go to the fort, he pulled his shorts down mid-thigh. I gave him a blow job, and as he finished he remarked, "Damn you're really good at that. We have to do this more often." As I walked away something inside me said, *enough is enough.* I wasn't going to allow this to happen ever again.

As I walked across the field back towards home, I noticed I had missed my curfew, so I knew I was in trouble. My mom was sitting on the couch with her beer and cigarette in her mouth. As I walked in the trailer mom said, "So you think your ass is grown huh? You don't pay no motherfucking bills in this goddamn house. When I say be in here before dark that's what the fuck I mean! I'm not playing with you!" Thankfully it was just words, so it was easy to brush off. My punishment for coming in late was I wasn't allowed to eat dinner, and I had to go straight to bed.

A few weeks went by without me seeing Scott in the trailer park or at the fort. Then, out of nowhere he appeared. It was late, and everyone was getting ready to head home. He kept staring at me, but I refused to make eye contact with him. One of the kids in the group asked him where he had been, and he said he had to work long shifts.

I looked at Tre' Quan and told him it was time to go. He responded, "Mom said I can stay at my friend's house." I was mad. How does he get to stay with a friend when he is constantly coming home late, drunk and/or high? I got up and stormed off, pissed at the double standard.

As I crossed the field to head home, I realized Scott was following me. He jogged and caught up. He asked me if I enjoyed last time, I responded, "No."

He started laughing and said, "Come on man, let's do it again."

I responded, "Na, I'm good." Scott started to get frustrated. As I got home, once again, I realized my mom wasn't there.

As I walked toward our steps, Scott said, "Let's walk over there and talk," and he nodded toward the abandoned trailer that was to the left of our trailer. I walked up the stairs as if I didn't hear him. He grabbed me firmly by the upper arm and led me toward the abandoned trailer. I noticed that Scott was breathing fast and he was sweating. He yanked open the rear door of the abandoned trailer, which faced the front of our trailer, and said, "Come on."

I looked at him and said, "No," as I attempted to free myself from him. He told me, "I'm not going to ask you again." Once up the stairs in the trailer, I looked around and noticed that there was no carpet on the floors and most of the windows were broken out. Scott said, "Lay on the ground on your stomach."

I looked at him and I straightened up and I said, "No!" He again yanked my arm in a downward motion and I again tried to pull away. I knew where this was going, and I knew at this point that I was strong enough to fight.

Scott expected me to just do what he said to do; it was apparent to me that he hadn't planned on me resisting. I started yelling, "Let me go!" At this point, frantic, he attempted to put his hand over my mouth. I wasn't scared this time. I felt as though I was in control. Scott started trying to shush me, and eventually he ran out the door. After this encounter I walked differently. I felt different. I started to take control of my life. My perception of my place in the world improved drastically.

Behind the Wheel

A fond memory I had with my mother shortly after this experience was of her teaching me how to drive. In my mind this was the next step in me becoming a man.

We were heading back home to Unionville, MD to visit family. I could barely see over the steering wheel, hence my nickname Shortman. Mom had to put items underneath me on the seat to prop me up so I could see over the dashboard. Her car at the time was a 1972 green Malibu Classic with an all-white roof. I was all over the road, and she kept telling me to slow down. This was exciting, and I grinned from ear to ear. I almost ran off the road a couple of times. I wanted to drive fast, but mom was very patient with me.

Where'd She Go?

As we finished up the school year and headed into the summer, our mom disappeared and left Tre' Quan and me with extended family members.

While with our cousins, we went to church, completed chores, and became attached to our new family. This was a stable environment, but we longed for our mother, and we missed her.

Emotionally, I felt torn because on one side our mother had abandoned Tre' Quan and me to go off and do whatever she felt she had to do. On the other side, we were in a safe home.

I was very street-smart, so I listened when the grownups would talk amongst themselves. Often times, they didn't know I was there. Sometimes, I'd hear them say negative things about our mom. No matter what she did or failed to do, I always had love and respect for her; I began to build resentment for Jaidyn because when mom left, she took him with her.

As soon as we got into a routine and became comfortable, mom showed back up, and we returned to Dreamland. She acted as if no time had passed, but it was evident that Tre' Quan had lost all respect for our mom by the way he responded to her. Each argument pushed him closer and closer to the streets.

While all of this was going on, on a parallel track I was trying to figure out what I was going to do to survive. I knew I wasn't going to be able to complete high school. I wasn't smart enough. Music, breakfast, and lunch kept me going to school, but I wanted to make money to help provide for my family.

At times, when mom was stressed about rent being due, she would just lie on the couch and cry. I didn't know what to do. Sometimes I would sit in my room and cry. Other times, when she was drunk, I would lie down beside her and hold her.

As the summer ended and we got back into the routine of the school year, the holiday season was fast approaching. I wasn't fond of holidays because we almost never could afford gifts to celebrate. On Christmas Eve, I went to bed hopeful that the next day when I woke up, I would have at least one gift.

The next morning when I got up, there was nothing under the Christmas tree; this alone wasn't abnormal. We didn't have any heat. Yet, our mother had her alcohol, which caused me to have a visceral response. I yelled at her about the situation and walked out of the trailer as I slammed the door behind me.

As I walked away from the stairs, I could hear mom as she ran across the floor. The door flung open and she was in my face in what seemed like seconds. As she went to hit me, I grabbed her by her shoulders and screamed, "No! You stupid bitch!" The look on her face was one of shock, and my words left her frozen in her tracks. I had never shown aggression. I had never been argumentative or disrespectful towards her.

As I saw her reaction, I too was shocked at my response, and I ran off into the woods. Once in the woods I threw myself on the ground. It was cold, the ground was covered in snow, and I lay there as I cried, disappointed in myself because I had disrespected my mother and called her out of her name.

I was upset with myself for allowing those emotions beneath the surface to get the better of me. It felt like an eternity as I lay on the ground, but eventually I got up and went home.

As I walked in the door, mom just looked at me. I was fully prepared for her to throw something at me or hit me with something. She didn't do anything; she just sat there. I think she could tell that I was already hurt more than she could have hurt me physically.

The Show Must Go On

I never asked myself why all of this was happening. It was just life as I knew it, and my focus was to get through each day. When I hit the bottom, the sunken place where I couldn't go any further, I attempted suicide. I was pretending to be ok and smiling to keep the family together, and to keep up appearances, yet on the inside I was broken.

At 13 years old, I was finishing up middle school. Tre' Quan had all but turned to gang life to get the things he felt he needed to survive. It is interesting how both of us could grow up in the same environment, witness the same things, and experience a lot of the same events, yet still feel so differently about them. I continued to seek out church opportunities because the truth is, though I was there for safety and food, both my mind and soul were being fed as well.

Fate would have it that I attended a Bible camp that was put on by a church, located in Suffolk, VA. In reality it was a missionary trip for those that came to the eastern shore.

While attending the Bible camp, I was picked up along with other kids from the neighborhood and driven to Dreamland II, where we were given the opportunity to do arts and crafts and learn about God's love, grace and mercy. At the end of the day we were all taken back to the trailer park and dropped off.

A couple of days into the Bible camp I got dropped off, and as I walked across the field, I saw a group of guys picking on Tre' Quan. Without hesitation, I knew it was time to roll up my sleeves and fight. No one was going to pick on my brother.

As I ran up to defend Tre' Quan, I realized rather quickly that he was taking part in his gang initiation. This was something I had been trying for years to protect him from. He was given the choice in this moment to either fight against them with me and lose his opportunity or he could team up with them, and they'd all beat me up.

I will never forget standing there, looking at this group (some teenagers and some adults). I thought to myself, *how did we get here,* as I looked to my brother whom I had protected his entire life. The fights we had been in flashed in my head, the times we were hungry, the times I had been molested and he lay feet away from me, the time we got our first Starter name-brand jackets, and times when my mother was being beaten and I had held him. All of those experiences flashed before me as I looked at him, seeing something different in him.

Before, when we fought others, Tre' Quan never hesitated. But at this moment, I saw him pause; he was hesitating, he was questioning and having an internal struggle. It all happened so fast, but there was so much to process in a short amount of time. I saw it in his eyes the instant he had made the decision. This person whom I loved dearly and whom I had given a lot for threw me away as if I was nothing. He decided that he was going to side with them and fight me.

Tre' Quan didn't have to say anything. It was in his actions as he threw the first punch knocking me on the ground. I started to fight back, but as I realized the gravity of what had just taken place, I just laid there and curled up as they kicked, punched and stomped me.

I was back in a familiar place. It was as if all of this was happening in slow motion. I stared into my brother's face and saw anger, resentment and rage. After they were done, they all walked away. I lay there soaked in blood, crying, not from the pain, but because I felt like I had failed. In a way though, hindsight being 20/20, I did my job. I protected my brother from being hurt.

Someone in the trailer park called 911, and police and EMS arrived. By the time my mother got there, EMS personnel had placed me on a stretcher and were loading me up into the ambulance. I had refused to talk to the police as I was taught. It honestly didn't matter anymore. Two officers tried to talk to me but grew frustrated when I wouldn't give them any information and walked off.

As my mother was told what happened, she got on the ambulance and looked at me and said, "You're going to be fine." Then she looked at the EMS personnel and told them, "I'll take him to the hospital if he needs to go." One of the EMS personnel attempted to speak with my mom off the ambulance, but there was no conversation to be had. The EMS personnel were concerned about the possibility of brain injury or a concussion from me being kicked and stomped in the head repeatedly.

Mom guaranteed them she would keep a close eye on me. Reluctantly, I was released into her care. As I listened to my mother arguing, I knew she was more worried about the medical bill than my well-being.

Scott and a couple of other guys helped carry me into the trailer that belonged to a friend of my mom, which was close by, and laid me on the couch. I'd lay there throughout the night in pain staring at the ceiling. Mom left and went back home and told me she'd be back in the morning to check on me.

The next morning word spread to my section leader, Robert (from the missionary event I had been attending), about what had happened to me. At the end of Bible camp, he came and found me at mom's friend's trailer.

I was lying on the couch, and when I realized it was him who had knocked on the door, I was glad to see him. He had been so kind to me. He asked how I was doing, and I told him I was alright. I was in pain, but it was more mental pain than physical.

I wondered why someone would care so much about me. Robert asked, "Can you walk?"

I replied, "Yes sir."

As we walked down the gravel driveway, he asked, "If you could leave all of this behind, would you?"

I didn't have to even think twice about my answer. "Yes," I said.

He replied, "Well if your mother will agree, then you can come and stay the summer with me and my family." I was going into the unknown, but the unknown was better than what I had experienced, and it couldn't have gotten any worse.

Robert and a few other people who attended the mission trip with him approached mom and asked if he could take me for the summer, and she replied, "Yes." I was so excited. Robert told me to pack some things and they'd pick me up the next day. When my mother said yes, I was glad to leave the misery behind. My mother wrote a note of permission on a piece of paper and off I went.

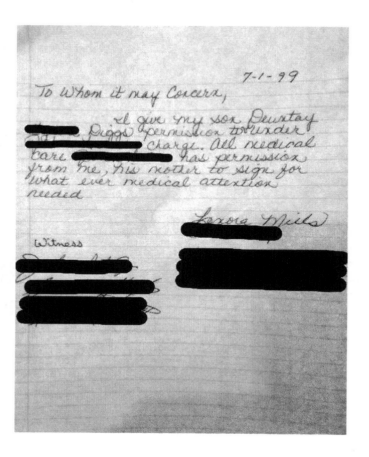

7-1-99

To Whom it may Concern,

I give my son Dwntay ███████ Piggs permission to under ███████ charge. All medical care ███████████ has permission from me, his mother to sign for what ever medical attention needed

███████████

Witness

███████████
███████████
███████████

Chapter Two

An Adventure

Sometimes you must go through a storm in order to be prepared for what is to come. Being betrayed by my brother led to the biggest change in my life. Two years before this I was going to commit suicide, and the thing that saved me was knowing I had to be there for my brothers.

There was a time when I didn't think there was anything in the world that would take me away from them. Yet here I was leaving it all behind without a second thought. The next day, Robert and a few others from the missionary trip came to pick me up. I didn't sleep much the night before because I was so excited. Finally, my opportunity had come.

On my first day while staying at the hotel, I asked Robert "What should I call you?"

He said, "Whatever you want."

When I arrived at the hotel, I walked through an alleyway and I noticed kids were jumping in a pool and having fun. I wanted to have fun too, so I ran and jumped in as well.

In my excited state I failed to realize that I couldn't swim. As I sank to the bottom I looked up while I patiently waited for someone to come rescue me. After being rescued, Robert would later joke, lovingly, that they had me for one day, and they almost lost me.

The next day I left the Eastern Shore, VA, and traveled to Gates County, NC. Robert, the man I would come to call Father, had a son Paul, who was about the same age as my youngest brother Jaidyn, and a wife Sarah.

As we took the long drive from the Eastern Shore to Suffolk, VA, I stared out the window, and I was excited about my new journey. *What were his wife and son going to be like? What kind of car would they have? What would their home look like?*

As we pulled into the church, I was beaming with joy to meet Sarah and Paul. Paul had just gone through a minor surgery and was in some pain and half asleep in the back seat; Sarah was overjoyed to meet me. At this point, Sarah had some time to adjust after she had received a call from Robert saying, "Honey I'm bringing home a 13-year-old kid."

It wasn't lost on me that, at the time, both Robert and Sarah were in their early 20's. Robert worked as a heating and air technician, and Sarah was a nurse. One of the first things we discussed upfront was that my job was to just be a kid and have fun.

Going to shop at the mall or Walmart was a new experience for me. Listening to country music, NASCAR, or being in close proximity to someone that displayed the battle flag of Robert E. Lee's army of northern Virginia was foreign. To me the flag stood for racism, but here I witnessed extended family display it and still treat me as one of their own. My belief system and what I had been taught was being challenged, which opened me up to other people's perspectives and reality over time.

As the summer was coming to an end, I started to miss my immediate family as well as my extended family. I was upset that no one reached out to me during my first summer in NC. As the summer came to an end and it was time to go back home, I wanted to stay, and Robert, Sarah and Paul wanted me to stay as well. We all quickly bonded over the summer and became a family.

The Visit

My mother, Tre' Quan, and Jaidyn got the opportunity to come out and see where I was living. During the visit I wanted my brothers to have the same opportunity that I had been given; I wanted them to stay. I had long moved past the pain from the fight, and though I didn't agree with what happened, there was a peace in my soul about it. Tre' Quan preferred to stay where he was, and mom wasn't going to let Jaidyn go because he was her baby and all she had left.

Before it was time for my mom and brothers to leave, she and I took a walk to discuss whether or not I was going to be able to stay. I could see it in her face as we spoke that she wanted me to come back home, but I pleaded with her to let me stay. I told her about many of my great experiences, how happy I was, and how nice Robert and his family had been to me.

Eventually, I pushed my mom to agree to allow me to stay. Mom signed the necessary paperwork to allow Robert and Sarah to place me in school. Looking back on that time, I feel like I was selfish for not taking into account how I made my mother feel. I can only imagine her thoughts as we dropped her and my brothers off and I rode away to begin a new path in life.

Learning the Basics

As it became time for the new school year to start, I was both nervous and excited. Once again, I had found myself in a small town where everyone knew each other. I thought to myself, *would the other kids like me? Would I fit in?* For the first day of school my confidence was high. I had new shoes, all my school supplies, and a new attitude. The issue was that I didn't truly have the foundation in education to be successful. Unlike the past when I would be the class clown to draw attention away from my lack of knowledge, I dared not do anything that would get me in trouble.

I was smart enough to know that I had a great family and opportunity, and I wasn't going to mess it up. My focus was to get good grades. I also began to realize that graduating was within my grasp if I put in the effort.

Sometimes there were concepts that other kids picked up in a class period that would take me a week or two to get. I really had to focus hard on studying certain topics to catch up. I learned fast that people don't know what you don't understand until you open your mouth and reveal it to them. I would fake it until I made it.

While sitting in class, I would breathe a sigh of relief when other students would ask what some would deem "stupid questions" because those questions helped me understand the material. Going into my freshman year of high school, I didn't understand sentence structure, verbs or pronouns. I hated math and writing. The only classes I liked were chorus, dance, and band.

In high school, I wanted to make everyone around me laugh. I learned that I had the ability to connect with people and relate to them. I hung out with everyone in high school. At this point, I knew what it felt like to be considered an "other" and to not be a part of something. I hung out with the "good ole boys," the "thugs" (as some would call them), the "smart people," the "goths," and other cliques: I had the ability to move throughout each group with ease and blend in. Despite all the reasons I had to fail, I was making it. The hard work was paying off.

Testing the Waters

During my freshman year of high school I realized that I had an attraction to the same sex. It was really just a fleeting thought that I found another guy attractive: a thought that scared me and I quickly suppressed it. This went against everything I was taught religiously. It was not normal, not natural. I hated myself for having had the thought, and I pushed it out of my mind.

I began to ask myself questions like, *did I have the thought because I had been molested by men?* I dared not share this thought with anyone. I had to find a female to date because that would fix everything.

As I was thrust into this new environment, this new way of life, this new culture, survival no longer was my main focus. There were many issues that were hidden beneath the surface that I had not dealt with. This new pace of life was unfamiliar to me, and it took some time to adjust. I had to keep moving forward, and, no matter what, I had to smile.

I had a hard time sleeping, and for years I would often have nightmares about being molested. Frequently, I would sit outside on the tailgate of Robert's truck and stare out across the field. He would come out and talk to me and ask what was wrong, but I dared not speak about it. Most times I would just say that everything was fine. My fear was that if I revealed that I had been sexually abused, then Robert and Sarah might think that I would do the same thing to their son. I did not want that stigma, and if that was true, then that also meant that I was going to be sent back.

I suspected that out of concern, and maybe some frustration, Robert and Sarah scheduled me to see a therapist. In my head I thought this was pointless. I knew from the moment I walked in the door that I wasn't going to open up to anyone. There was no way that I was going to do anything to ruin my life as it was.

I looked at the therapist as a threat, and so I sat in the chair for the first couple of visits studying her and vaguely answering questions. Eventually, on the ride home one afternoon, Robert said, "Son, if you're not going to talk then we don't need to keep doing this."

I replied with, "Yes sir," as I looked out of the window. By this time, the therapist hadn't gained my trust. I hated how after we spoke, I would sit out in the lobby and she would talk to my parents without me. I had my suspicions that she was telling them what I had said during our visit.

At the next visit I figured I'd talk if that would make Robert happy. The next visit to the therapist began, and I jumped right in and I told the therapist one of the things I struggled with the most, was not being able to see my biological mother and brothers more often.

I didn't have to make anything up, but I knew this was a point of contention with Robert and Sarah, not because they didn't want to accommodate me, but because it wasn't an option fiscally. I knew they couldn't afford it, but it doesn't mean that the feelings I had just disappeared.

Like before, after the appointment I was asked to sit out in the chair, and my parents went in. On the way home in the car, my suspicion was confirmed because Robert started explaining why I couldn't visit my mom and brothers regularly. I stopped talking to the therapist, and the sessions ended.

Shortly thereafter, I had an incident where I brought up wanting to visit my mom on the Eastern Shore. Not only would it have been a financial burden, but it would have also been time consuming. One of the family members told me that I had to make a choice between staying or being with my biological family.

I will never forget how Robert and Sarah dealt with it. They were upset that this had happened to me. They made it clear to me that the family member was wrong, and that it was not how they felt. Seeing how they defended me was one of the factors that helped ease some of the anxiety and stress I had about being sent back.

The Ugly Truth

In this new family, I dared not talk back to my parents or disobey them. Internally, I constantly weighed every decision or action, fearing that it could be the issue that would send me back. I would hear Robert and Sarah talk about what a good kid I was because I always did the chores as asked. As time went on though, I got a little lazy with it.

They did everything that they could to let me know they loved me. I appreciated it and recognized it. In the beginning, I often wondered what Robert and Sarah's motives were. I was so grateful for everything they were doing for me, but I couldn't figure out why they were doing it all. I couldn't believe that people could be this kind. What did they hope to get out of helping me? I came to learn as time went on that they just wanted me to be successful and to pay it forward.

An issue that I wasn't prepared to deal with was racism from the people in the community that looked like me. Some black people felt like I had betrayed my race since I lived with white people.

Racism and prejudice were things that I navigated throughout high school, but my thought process was challenged. My upbringing had taught me that this was an issue that only white people had. It was interesting how some people challenged the idea of a black male being raised by white people with comments like, "It just don't sit right." Most of the critics, however, never opened their homes to any black children, male or female, in the foster care system.

When I stood behind my family, if we went to a restaurant or event, people did not think that I was with them. Often, I would be asked how I would like to pay for something or I'd be stopped and not allowed to continue with my family because I didn't look like them. I'd patiently wait for Robert to turn around and address the issue. Sometimes he would say, "Son you need to walk in front of us so this doesn't happen." Race wasn't something that we thought about in our family, but once outside, the world made sure to bring us back to reality every chance it had. We would make jokes or laugh about it and then continue on.

I once had a fellow student in high school call me a nigger while we were eating lunch in the cafeteria. He told me he was going to hang me and drag me behind his truck. I flipped the table in the lunch room and went after him as he took off down the hallway. Although his friends put him up to saying this racist comment, they weren't there to protect him. I just knew when Robert and Sarah were notified by the school that I was going to be in trouble. One might ask, "How did you know if you were in trouble with your parents?" If my full name was called out, then I knew. I might have gotten my ear pulled a couple of times as well, maybe a timeout, but it was rare. In this case, Robert and Sarah both understood my reaction and were supportive.

Brothers Regardless of Blood

Paul, Robert and Sarah's son, and I had a very close relationship. He never complained about me being a part of his family. In fact, when people questioned us being brothers, he would get mad. It was as if he didn't see color like others did. Over the years we grew to be very close.

There were very few times that you would see one of us without the other. He never used the phrases "My mom" or "My dad." It was "Our parents."--truly unconditional love. These moments taught me that family was not necessarily about blood, but more about the love that we had for one another.

There was nothing that he could do wrong in my eyes. Sometimes we'd get mad at each other, and he'd hit me. Robert would say, "Hit him back. Don't allow him to do that." I would never have thought of doing it, though. In reality, he helped to ease a void that was there from missing Tre' Quan and Jaidyn. There was a comfort in having a brother to look after.

I was also blessed with an extended family and lots of new cousins. Just like being on the Eastern Shore, my cousins, Paul, and I all played at our grandparent's house out in the country, running, laughing and enjoying our time together during holidays. We ate everything that we could get our hands on. I was treated as if I had been born into the family and there was never any sign of awkwardness or distrust. This acceptance was a true reflection of humanity at its best.

"Pretty Hurts"

One of the methods that Robert and Sarah did to boost my self-image, which was still very low, was to set me up to have surgery on my ear. There was a cyst on my right ear that pushed my ear outwards. From my earliest memories, and well into my teenage years, kids called me Dumbo or made fun of me for having big ears.

Sarah took me to an ear, nose and throat specialist. The doctor decided to go in and take the cyst out. As she explained the procedure, I was told my ear was going to be cut off and then put back on. For a second, my excitement about fixing my ear went away. I thought to myself, *what if she can't put it back on, then what?* Sarah assured me that everything was going to be okay, and we had a good laugh.

What they found when they went to go and operate was that the cyst was benign and that it was a sack of fluid that wrapped around to the back of my head. After the operation was completed, my ear was sewn back on and my ear laid flat against my head.

Heavy Weight

A couple of years into staying with Robert and Sarah, Robert got hurt, and when he could not work, money got tight. Even with the financial hardship, there was never any mention of sending me back because I was an added expense.

We got help from the church family to get food and pay bills. God and church were a huge part of our lives and the focal point of my upbringing as a teenager. It was awesome to see the support, concern and love from the congregation in our time of need.

Along the way, each time life threw a reason at Robert and Sarah to get rid of me or send me back, they didn't entertain it. For me, there was something in my gut that wouldn't let the notion go. My feelings of fear, the anxiety of being sent back or having to be the perfect kid were all self-inflicted.

I found it much easier to open up more to Sarah than Robert due to the experiences I'd had as a child. I suspected that this had to be frustrating to him because he had been the one who had initiated bringing me into the family. Still, I was guarded. Out fear, I never gave them an opportunity to address my concerns of being expendable.

One issue I opened up to Sarah about was my struggle with not knowing my biological father. She asked, "Why do you need him?" I explained that I wanted to know if I looked like him or if I spoke like him. She replied, "Okay, let's see what we can find." We did a search for him, but we had very limited information to go off of. The initial search went nowhere, but Sarah's willingness to help meant the world to me.

Academic Decision

By the time I had the opportunity to do sports, I had missed out on the basics as a kid. I still enjoyed as I watched Paul play basketball and baseball, though. It just so happened that his baseball coach was a Virginia Military Institute (VMI) Alumnus. Up to this point, I had prepared to join the military. I felt as though I wasn't smart enough to get accepted into college. Going into my junior year of high school, I started speaking with recruiters for the armed services. I had my mind set on going into the Marine Corps, much to the dissatisfaction of my parents.

Going into the Marine Corp meant that I'd have financial stability. It meant that I was going to have the ability to defend myself. It also meant that I would be able to go back and take care of my biological family. I still hadn't lost my goal of making it and being able to give back to my mother and my two brothers that I'd left behind.

Like many parents during this time, Sarah knew the Iraq War was fast approaching and felt like I should go to college before joining the military. After Paul's baseball practice one day, his coach pulled me aside and said, "If you are going into the military, then you should become an officer. You'd make more money that way." He talked further talked to me about VMI and other service academies and mentioned I could get military experience and my degree at the same time. Without knowing much, I heard "Money," and blurted out, "Sign me up!"

I began preparing for the ACT and the SAT. I knew that this was going to be a major feat because I had a hard time taking tests. I took the SAT the first time and did poorly. The second time I took the test, I did better, but I learned a new test taking skill. I learned that if I took the test backwards from the last page to the first page that it calmed my anxiety. I went on to take the ACT and scored exceptionally well. I was doing it; I was becoming someone in spite of all the reasons I had to fail. It wasn't lost on me at the time that, by God's grace, Robert and Sarah had taken a chance on me, and I recognized that the opportunity was leading me to great places.

As my ego and confidence were building, one day at the end of school while I walked to the bus ramp, I jumped in on my first rap battle and won. I had no clue what I was doing. I threw something up against the wall and it stuck. I thought I was king of the hill, but I soon learned that my success was going to be short lived, as I entered the next battle and was torn to shreds. I licked my wounds and kept moving. But I learned a valuable lesson: No one stays on top forever. Be kind to those that you pass on the way up because eventually you'll see them on the way down. A week or so went by, and I stumbled, almost throwing my new-found success off track.

A Big Mistake

I got off the bus and waited for Paul. We walked home, got a snack, and started our homework. Robert and Sarah came home, and we had family time, which consisted of dinner and watching TV.

There was a knock at the back door, and I heard someone ask Robert, "Can Deuntay come outside?" He told them, "Sure." It wasn't unusual for kids from the neighborhood to come to play a pick-up game of basketball. I got my shoes on and walked outside. As I was standing outside, Dennis, one of the guys who had been over to the house multiple times, approached me and said, "I heard you wanted to fight me."

I responded with, "That's not true," as I created space between us. I then noticed that Keith, another guy I was familiar with, was walking up behind me. I turned with my back to the house.

As Keith walked towards me at a fast pace he yelled, "I know you've been hitting on my girl!"

In my head I thought, *Bullshit. I have no idea what you heard, but it wasn't true.* I had just enough time to look over and see Ray and Brian, who were brothers, coming up behind Dennis. I knew what time it was, and if I was going down, I was taking as many of them as I could with me.

As I looked back, Keith was the closest to me, and with all my might I punched him in the nose. This essentially took him out of the fight. I then went into a fit of rage and completely lost all control. Dennis backed off rather quickly. I was later told that I had slammed Ray's head into the neighbor's grill, and that I pushed Sarah as her and Robert attempted to get me off Brian.

What got me to this place was my inability to communicate and having kept so many issues bottled up because I was suspicious of everyone.

Afterwards, the police were called. I pressed charges and there were counter charges against me for assault because I had broken Keith's nose. Keith's father told Robert that kids are kids but wanted to know who was going to pay the doctor's bills for his son.

In my mind at the time, I was absolved of any guilt because they had come onto my property with the intent of doing me harm. When it came time for court, I sat there feeling like I had the case won before it even started. There were four of them and one of me, case closed. They got what they deserved.

After testifying and both sides rested, the judge handed down his sentence to the four guys. As I sat there, I smiled as they were told that they were going to have to do some time in jail.

The judge then addressed me. As I stood, he stated there was no doubt in his mind that they had gotten what they asked for, but I was more than willing to give it to them. He also said that I had stepped out of being the victim and that I became the aggressor. He sentenced me to serve time as well but didn't hold me responsible for restitution for Keith's broken nose. I was shocked.

Robert stood up and defended me, as he explained to the judge my history. He told the judge that I was a great kid with a lot going for me. He talked about how he had rescued me and saved me from the situation that I had come from. He said that he did not want the courts to take away my chances of going to VMI.

The judge acknowledged Robert and gave the stipulation that if I served my time and didn't get into any other trouble within a year, then my charges would be expunged from my record. The judge assured my dad that if I were given the opportunity to go to VMI, this would not prevent me from doing so.

We set up the date and time to report to the county jail. As it quickly approached, I talked tough like I wasn't afraid. I could see the fear and concern in my parents' eyes. I assured them that I was going to be okay.

When they dropped me off, I was patted down and searched. I changed my clothes and put on the county jail-issued uniform. I'd heard all the typical stuff about jail: Be tough, don't let anyone push you around, stand your ground, be careful in the showers. As all those thoughts were going through my head, I was determined to make it through this experience without any issues.

The first night I walked into my cell, the door opened, I stepped in, was given a blanket, and the door slid closed, clanging shut. I broke down crying, quietly that is. I remember saying to myself, *never again*. Never again would I be in this predicament. Never again would I allow someone else to control my emotions or to make me lose control. I lay there and thought about what I could have done better and asked myself where I wanted to go in life. I knew I was in control of my own destiny. The question I asked myself was whether I was going to break the cycle or give up and allow myself to be just another casualty of my circumstances.

The next morning, I got up, brushed my teeth and went to take a shower. I was nervous about the shower, but because we were under age, we weren't allowed to go to the shower by ourselves. A corrections officer watched over us. That made me somewhat more comfortable. At breakfast, one of the inmates said, "Give me your food," and I just looked back at him. I noticed that the other guys that I'd gotten into the fight with had their food taken. I ignored the inmate and kept eating. For the remainder of my stay I was left alone.

Over the short period of time that we were locked up, the other inmates found out what had happened and teased the other guys. While in the day room, I made a pact with Keith that we were cool and that we were moving on with our lives.

When school started, no one messed with me. Rumors got around that I could fight. Part of me felt as though I should have fought earlier, and then I wouldn't have had to deal with so many issues. Part of me felt like fighting wasn't the best way to handle everything. It wasn't the right way to go about getting respect. I didn't want to be feared. I just wanted to be left alone.

New Found Respect

Three years into staying with Robert and Sarah, my extended biological family found out that my mother had given me away to strangers. The family was shocked, hurt and upset because they had been lied to. They couldn't understand why my mother did what she did.

I eventually told my aunt just how bad things were as a child. She said they knew things were bad, but they just didn't know how bad. On a brief family vacation to Orlando, FL my entire extended biological family stopped and picked me up. Though much time had passed, it felt like we just picked up where we left off.

As I began to sort through some of my childhood and what had happened in my life up to that point, I had believed that no one in the family cared about me. My perception was that they had abandoned me based on their lack of contact with me. The reality was that they had no idea. What I learned during this time was that before jumping to conclusions or letting your emotions take control, make sure you have all the facts first.

I would later learn that my aunt had asked to take my brothers and me to raise. Our mother had refused, though. I also learned that mom had lied for years about my whereabouts when she would encounter family members. Gaining this knowledge shaped how I dealt with conflict going forward.

On the way back from Orlando, FL my family was just waiting for me to say that I didn't want to go back to Robert and Sarah's, and they would have kept driving. It was very hard for them to leave me behind, but knowing where I was, and that I was being taken care, of made it a bit more bearable.

Lurking Beneath the Surface

As the summer came to an end, I was going into my senior year of high school. During my junior year, I tried out for drum major and was selected. This was significant because I was not from North Carolina, and somehow, someway I had earned the respect of not only the band director but my peers as well.

Our band camp was held at Ferrum College in Virginia. While there I met a guy by the name of RJ from another high school band. He and I enjoyed hanging out after practices. We both couldn't wait to hangout and talk about our day and about life. It was a bromance. On the last night of band camp, RJ snuck over to my dorm and asked if he could stay the night. I said, "Sure."

He said, "I'm going to miss you."

I said, "I feel the same way." He asked if he could write me, and I said, "Absolutely." I gave him my address.

As I lay on the bed on my back, and he laid on the floor, we just talked most of the night and eventually he asked, "Can I get up there with you?"

"Sure," I responded.

He said, "Little spoon or big spoon?"

I said, "Neither, I'd prefer a fork." We busted out laughing as he called me a goofball. Then I started to have feelings that I didn't want to have. Feelings that I had been taught were wrong. So, I turned over and faced the wall. I closed my eyes tightly and I started praying, "God help me." As RJ puts his arms over me, strangely it just felt right and everything connected. I turned over and I asked, "Are you gay?"

He answered, "I don't know."

I looked at him and he said, "I don't want to be, I can't be. I would lose my family." He turned over and started to cry. I held him as we fell asleep.

I woke up the next day, and RJ was gone, but had left a note. I got dressed quickly, and I ran down the hall, down the stairs, and across the field to his dorm. He and his band were gone. I had so much that I wanted to say to him, but I didn't know if I was going see him again or if he would actually write me.

I walked back to my room, packed my stuff and headed for the bus to go back home. Instead of sitting up front, I sat in the back seat so I could have a little more privacy. I opened the letter and started to read it.

RJ told me that he had dreamed of a night like the night we shared and that it was the first time he had had that experience. He went on to say that he had fallen for me but was afraid of rejection and couldn't say it. He said he would be willing to give up everything to be with me. I read the letter twice, and I had a rush of emotions that were all over the place. I kept asking myself, *what had I done?* I also knew by this point that if I came out as being gay that it would be the end of my relationship with my family. I decided that I would forget this had ever happened. I had done so once before, and I could do it again. But I found myself checking the mailbox often.

One day a letter came from RJ, and I was so excited. In the letter he caught me up on all the things that were going on in his life since I had last seen him. I wrote him back and had a secretary at my high school send the letter for me. After a few more letters came to the house, Robert grew suspicious. He told me to ask RJ not to send any more letters, thus ending my ability to stay connected.

While at our very last band competition at Cary High School, I randomly saw RJ. It was such an awesome moment when our eyes locked. We gave each other a huge hug and hung out the rest of the night. Though I had dated two females up to this point, neither relationship came close to the connection that I had with RJ, which led me to speak about it with my high school's nurse during my senior year.

I can't explain why I chose this nurse, but I walked in, checked the room, made sure we were alone, and just started talking. I told her about how I thought I was gay, and I explained about RJ. I spoke to her about not wanting to go to hell and about hating myself for the feelings that I had.

"How do I get rid of this?" I asked her.

She looked at me and said, "You are perfect the way you are." I began crying.

"It's going to be okay," she said. I asked her if she was going to contact my parents, and she said that our conversation would stay between us. She said, "I have a friend that I think can help you."

A couple of days later I was introduced to the nurse's friend in the nurse's office. I later sat down with this gentleman during lunch. I had met this man before. I saw the red flags almost instantly.

He asked me if I was 18, and he asked me if I was able to hang out with him outside of school. I responded by telling him that I was 17 and that us hanging out was never going to happen because my parents would never allow it. I met with him a couple more times, but nothing inappropriate ever happened. Thinking back, I only tolerated the uneasiness I felt around him and the way he complimented me on what I was wearing or the way I looked, because I wanted to learn so desperately what it meant to be gay.

I knew speaking with my parents about the feelings I was experiencing wasn't a good idea. Based off religious beliefs, and like RJ, I too had a gut feeling that it would get me kicked out of my immediate family. In the few times I had the conversations with the nurse's friend, I would glean as much as I could.

Often parents fail to realize that when they shut the door on their children, the world will open another, and it very well may not be the best one.

A Silver Lining

As time went on, Robert, Sarah and I spoke about adoption. But if I were adopted, I would have to change my last name, and that was not something I wanted to do. I also learned through the process that my biological mom would have to agree to it. I couldn't bring myself to hurt my mother in that way. So, it was placed on the back burner and left there.

As a child, my unattainable dream was graduating from high school. It was a dream, an aspiration. It was not something that I had thought I would actually be able to accomplish. So, there I was in my senior year, and I had received my acceptance letter to VMI. I made it and was going to graduate. How did this happen? I realized that I didn't make it to that moment alone. Both the good and bad experiences had ushered me into this moment, and I was living.

As I walked across the graduation stage, I couldn't believe that I had done it. As I lifted my hands and looked towards the sky, my classmates cheered. It was my way of saying thank you to God for blessing me.

I was so happy as I looked out into the crowd and saw Robert, Sara and Paul. I knew that without them this day wouldn't have come. Part of me was hurting because I wanted my mom and brothers to be there to celebrate as well, but I had to let this sadness go and live in the moment.

Chapter Three

Off to College

When I think of the Virginia Military Institute (VMI), I think of the statement, "It is a great place to be from, but not a great place to be at." To me, VMI initially was an ambitious, lofty idea that was unattainable; but with the right support system and resources, I found myself conquering my self- imposed limitations.

As I struck out on my journey to VMI, I really didn't know much about the Institute. From the bits of knowledge I obtained, I knew I had many challenges to face ahead. I was determined not to give up and to do whatever was necessary to graduate and become an officer in the military. I was very nervous about academics, but I knew that my physical fitness and ability to catch on fast would help me.

I learned VMI has its own language. It's steeped in rich tradition, and in order to be successful, you have to find a way to balance the three-legged stool: academics, military and athletics. I learned rather quickly the ability to multitask was essential to success.

Before my cadetship began, I went to an open house to tour the campus and to spend a night in the barracks. When I went, the Rats were broken out, which means the freshmen had received their class privileges and were considered 4th Class cadets.

"Rat" is the name given to freshmen who matriculate at VMI. The Rat-Line is a unique tradition in which new cadets walk at rigid attention with their chin tucked in, commonly referred to as straining, along a prescribed route whenever they are inside barracks. At any time, a Rat can be stopped and tested by upper-class cadets on institutional knowledge, and should he or she fail, the Rat will be made to do push-ups.

While visiting, I got a very different sense of what VMI was since I did not see the Rat-Line in effect. There was no one straining, no one doing push-ups, no one yelling. The atmosphere pre-breakout vs post-breakout was very different. As I sat and spoke with my host cadet, he asked me "Why do you want to come to my school?"

Without missing a beat, I looked at him and replied, "I want to be a part of something bigger than myself."

He smiled and said, "We shall see."

While I was on my visit, I was introduced to Colonel Brodie, the regimental band director. From the moment I met him, I felt admiration and respect for him. His demeanor was so different than everyone else I had met. It was apparent that he marched to the beat of his own drum, pun intended. He'd light up a room when he entered it with his comical sense of humor and charisma. When he learned that I played the trombone, he was very excited, and I left the visit pledging that I was going to be in Band Company.

Robert, Sarah and Paul drove me from Gates County, NC to Lexington, VA to drop me off at VMI for the beginning of the school year. The drive there was scenic with mountains, hills and open fields with livestock.

During the drive there, Robert asked me if I had ever seen mountain cows. He said that the cows could stand on the side of the mountain and still look like they were standing level because two legs were shorter than the others. I looked at him and thought, *What?? Really??* He started to laugh and said, "You are so gullible. You'll believe anything!" I'd never really been up close to cows, so I thought that was weird, but, hey, what did I know. As we pulled up to VMI, I could see that Robert and Sarah were proud of me, but they didn't really want to leave me. Eventually, it was time to say goodbye, and I was onto a new adventure.

Laying the Foundation

Even though the registration process was organized, it seemed chaotic. People were running around grabbing uniforms and registering for classes. I was issued my Rat Bible, which held the knowledge of the Institute, the corps structure, and gave me the information I would need to be successful as I navigated the Rat-Line.

With VMI came a whole new vocabulary. The first time I heard the term "Rat Bible," I thought that was blasphemous. You don't call something the Bible unless it is the actual Bible. The humidity was high on campus, and it seemed like everything was uphill. A short while later I was stripped of my regular clothes, which are called "civvies" and was put into "gym dyke" clothing, which is a name for VMI workout gear.

Next, I, along with my fellow matriculants, was ushered down to the trunk room where our civilian clothes were stored. At this time, we all started meeting one another and forming bonds, and we began the journey of becoming a class. After the administrative tasks were taken care of, the fun began.

As I was standing in formation with men and women that I barely knew, we were learning what it meant to be at attention. It was easy for me coming from marching band in high school. As I stood there, with the sun beating down on me, I heard a drumbeat and thought to myself *what is going on?* But I dared not break the position of attention to figure it out. Then, out of my peripheral vision, I could see two lines of upperclassmen marching ever so slowly to the beat of a drum.

They were wearing grey blouses and white pants with a scowl on their faces. As the upperclassmen marched in, some of the Corps formed up and yelled things like, "You're about to get it, Rats!" The formations were arranged by company, and we were lined up such that we were facing each other with a huge gap in the middle. As the upperclassmen took their time marching between the formations, I thought to myself, *why are they so mad? Fix it, Jesus! Well I guess I'd be mad too if I had to wear wool out here in this heat.*

With precision, the upperclassmen stopped with the beat of the drum and faced outwards. Their facial expressions were harsh and their eyes were cold. I could feel the anxiety and fear of my classmates as we all stood together. This moment is known as meeting your cadre, and it sets the tone of the Rat-Line and what is expected at VMI. "Rats meet your cadre," rang out through the barracks. Like a pack of rabid wolves, the cadre ran into the formation and started working us out, yelling and screaming. I realized rather quickly that life had prepared me for this.

During this ordeal, which is also known as the "shark attack", I learned that I was okay with it, while other people that had never been screamed at before were in shock. It was apparent that some immediately began questioning their decision to attend VMI. In my mind, it was just screaming. My mom did that all the time, so it was nothing new to me. It was at this point that I began to understand that my negative experiences growing up were going to help me navigate the Rat-Line a little more easily than some others.

What I also noticed at the time was that we were all dressed the same, and we were all treated the same. As the week continued, I went through many training activities, endured lots of physical training, and got the dreaded Rat-haircut, which means I didn't have any hair.

No Pressure

One of the most important things I came to understand as I learned about the history of VMI, and what was expected of me, was the Honor Code. The Honor Code is one of the most important pillars at VMI. "A Cadet will not lie, cheat, steal, nor tolerate those who do." If you violate the Honor Code, you can and will be kicked out of school, and your name is not to be mentioned in barracks ever again. This act brings shame upon your Dyke-Line, your family and yourself.

When a cadet has broken the Honor Code, you are awakened in the middle of the night to the sounds of drums, and the experience is jarring. For this very reason one could leave anything from money to equipment lying around, and it would stay right where you left it. It doesn't matter if it was at the gym, the barracks or any of the buildings on post.

While a Rat, you're next to nothing at VMI; it seems as though the world hates you. Each Rat receives a mentor, called a "Dyke," who is a senior. Some seniors have two Rats to mentor, and some only choose one. Their purpose is to coach you through the Rat-Line, to teach you everything you need to know to be successful at VMI. Their room is a safe haven from the chaos in barracks. Like many things at VMI, the ordeal of choosing a Rat is steeped in tradition and is very important.

Once a Rat is chosen, he/she becomes a part of and represents the coveted Dyke-Line, which includes all of those VMI cadets who came before you.

<u>Reasons to Give Up</u>

As time went on at VMI, I realized, almost immediately that the concerns I had with academics were going to be an issue. Robert and Sarah wanted me to do computer science or work towards some type of degree in engineering. They believed that this would set me up for success after I graduated.

I felt like I was not smart enough, nor did I possess the skill set or desire to work in any of those fields. Initially going into computer science, I thought that I would be taught how to turn on the computer. I could type, and I thought, *this is going to be easy.* I understood Microsoft Word. I did not know that I was going to be taking courses like discrete mathematics. What I learned quickly was that I was still behind academically for various reasons.

One issue that needed to be addressed was my being diagnosed with ADHD. I discovered that there was a strong possibility that taking medication would prevent me from getting a scholarship in the Marine ROTC program, so I was determined to learn how to manage it myself.

When you are good at something, you tend to want to focus on it. Some of my favorite times were when I was doing physical training or learning military maneuvers. My worst times were when I was sitting in the classroom. There were many occasions when I just fell asleep because it felt like I was so far out of my skill set and my ability to comprehend what was being taught. It was mentally exhausting at times.

The study skills I had learned that helped me successfully navigate high school weren't strong enough to be successful at VMI, and I had given up on myself. I'd gotten to this place where I thought, *I'm going to focus on what I do best.* I would focus on the military side.

My academic advisor Col. Piegari and I had a meeting in his office. As we discussed my academic failure, he told me that I was not cut out for VMI. He stated that it wasn't the place for me and that I should probably start looking for somewhere else to go. I was so angry as I left his office.

As I walked back to barracks, I got angrier with each step I took. *Who the hell did he think he was to tell me to start looking for somewhere else to go? How dare he speak to me that way.* For the first time in my life, I realized that the world didn't care about my experiences growing up as a child. It really didn't matter. What the world wanted to know was could I perform? Could I meet the standards? I learned that if I could not, then I would be brushed to the side and the cycle would keep going.

I thought to myself, *I'm going to show you. I'm going to turn this around and I'm going to graduate.* I had almost flunked out of computer science, and I had to do something to be able to come back after break. I knew that if I got suspended due to academics, I would not be coming back.

I changed my major of choice. I wanted to go into psychology, but the major was full at the time. I ended up studying History and focusing on Middle Eastern studies, specifically the Palestinian-Israeli conflict. I figured when I was deployed, at least this would allow me to understand the region and its people.

In studying history, I realized I had yet another obstacle because I had to know how to write. While I could write, I knew that I wasn't at the collegiate level, but I was determined to learn and become successful.

Another academic requirement that plagued me was that I needed to learn a language. I attempted Spanish, but I was not interested. I tried learning German, but I couldn't form the correct pronunciations with my mouth. I tried French, but I was terrible at it. I got to Arabic, and it was just right. One of the things that was natural for me with Arabic was reading from right to left instead of left to right.

As I improved academically, I later learned that Col. Piegari was wise beyond my comprehension. He knew I needed a challenge and a push. He was right. Without our tough talk, I would not have graduated from VMI.

When I realized the trickery he played on me, as I sat in my barracks room one evening almost a year later, all I could do was laugh. Even when I doubted myself, he saw the potential in me. I learned quickly at VMI that I didn't have time to be offended. I didn't have time to sit on the sidelines with my feelings hurt.

Though there were many who helped me to succeed academically, Teri B., Rose Mary S., Elena A. and Thomas D. all had a profound impact on my success. These faculty members mentored me, listened to my concerns, and helped me to keep things in perspective.

Inside the Castle

As the Rat-Line progressed, things were increasingly more and more difficult both academically and inside barracks. Inside barracks, there were just the essentials: no television, no air condition, and in the winter the heat came from radiators that made all kinds of sounds.

I had a rack, a wall locker, a desk, and hay. The rack is a cot that has legs which fold down on either side to create a bed. The hay is a thin mattress that is issued to you during matriculation and goes with you when you graduate.

As soon as I woke up in the morning, I would take care of my hygiene and then the hay was rolled tight and kept together with two straps. At first, it was a struggle to get the straps on the hay, but over time a cadet can do it with his/her eyes closed. Next, I'd place my rack in the corner with my roommate's, and finally the hay was placed in front of the racks in a line with the blankets folded and placed neatly on the top.

Most mornings, going from the 4th stoop down to the 1st stoop of barracks was easy because upperclassmen were sleeping, but coming back into barracks, around lunch, was a daring adventure during the Rat-Line. Rats knew that third classmen (sophomores) were lurking at the stairwells just waiting to drop them for not having a pristine uniform or for not being able to recite the knowledge of the Institute.

While a few of my Brother-Rats (classmates) would shy away and hang out in academic buildings, I would enter barracks, and I enjoyed the cat-and-mouse game. I figured if I didn't know something, I could only be pushed until I couldn't do push-ups anymore.

Sometimes, instead of being asked questions about institutional knowledge, I'd be asked, "Are you a football player or a permit?" Because most black cadets played football or were on a sports team, I was asked this question. Based solely off the color of my skin and my physique, I was put into this box. I would respond, "No, sir. Is it because I'm black, sir?" The response I would receive varied. Sometimes there was stumbling of words and a response of "I didn't mean it like that," or a smirk and a response with, "Well you're in the 1%! Get out of here, Rat!"

As my freshman year went on, and I had all of these new experiences, I began to try to figure out who Deuntay Diggs truly was and wanted to become. I don't think I had ever thought about that before. It was my first time away from my parents. I was off on my own. It was my opportunity to create my space for myself and figure out what I wanted to do with my life.

Learning Who I Am

As I was going through the Rat-Line, I began to come to terms with being gay. It was interesting for me because there was no going back once I had acknowledged it within myself. The concern that I had, was that I was coming out in a conservative environment, a rigid environment. I wondered what my family was going to think, and there couldn't have been a worse time to start thinking about this and trying to navigate the whole coming-out experience.

As I began to come to terms with my sexuality, I was very careful with what I said and how I presented myself. Often times people will say, "You can be gay, but the world doesn't need to know." Ironically, these same people will then ask questions such as: Who are you chatting with? Who are you talking to on the phone? Who are you going to meet? Do you have a girlfriend? When you say "No" to any of these questions or provide vague answers, then there are follow up questions.

As I tried to field these questions, one lie lead to the next, and before I knew it, I couldn't remember the first lie. Call me crazy, but in a place where I took to heart the Honor Code, I wasn't going to be deceitful. I didn't want to have to say I was going to see a girl when I was going to see a guy. I also didn't want to have to change male names to female names just to get by.

My intent is not to bash, shame or look down on anyone who used or is currently using these tactics. We all take different paths in life, and what works for some may not work for others. It is a personal decision, and some may need to do so to protect themselves. Each person must do what is best for them in the given circumstances.

The questions I asked and answered for myself were: *Does self-preservation give me the right to lie? Does going along with the status quo to get where I want to be, or to get what I want make it right? Once I obtain my goal or get to the finish line, will I be proud of myself?* In the midst of the chaos and questions, I was calm, and I knew it was time.

My Brother-Rats and I sat out on the parade deck in front of barracks after a company exercise as we were getting instruction for the next day. We were going into the weekend, and I was excited because that meant that most of the upperclassmen were going to be out of barracks.

After supper roll call (SRC), we marched down, ate dinner and then formed up and marched back up to barracks. We fell out and strained back to our rooms. Once we were left alone for the night, I looked out of my door window to see if the coast was clear. I didn't want to have to deal with cadre or the annoying third classmen.

As I exited the room, I strained while I ran down to Susan's room. Once there, we laughed, joked and hung out. From what I had seen from my classmates, Susan had a heart of gold and loved to help people. She also had an awesome personality, so I was drawn to her naturally.

Eventually, while hanging out, I told her, "I think I'm bisexual." I waited to see her reaction. But much to my surprise, she just said, "Okay," and shrugged it off as if she didn't care. I didn't know what was supposed to happen, but I didn't think that was the typical response. Without missing a beat, I said, "Well I think I'm actually gay but don't tell anybody." She had the same response just like previously.

I was on Cloud Nine. I had announced it finally, and it felt amazing. A huge weight was lifted off of my shoulders. As I left her room and strained back to mine, I felt a rush of excitement like I could conquer the world. As I got back to my room, I walked in and sat down.

As I sat there, I immediately began to question myself. What was I thinking, and why had I opened my mouth? It felt right, but was it truly? What if it was just a phase? Did I misread her body language? Was she okay with it? Eventually, I prepared for bed, and as I lay in my rack, I began to think. What was my future going to hold?

"I Don't Wanna Fight"

The next day I woke up, and it was business as usual. Get up, get dressed, roll your hay and then head to your Dyke's room to complete whatever tasks/chores had been assigned. My Dyke was easy on me. I just had to throw his trash away and roll his hay. Next, I'd walk out to breakfast roll call (BRC), with my Dyke, which meant I didn't have to strain.

While sitting at the table with my breakfast, I could immediately tell something was off with a few of my Brother-Rats. By this time, I had learned baselines for behavior. When they didn't think I was paying attention, I could feel their gaze as they stared at me.

The all-familiar sound echoes through Crozet Hall, "You're done Rats." As we got up and threw away our trash, one of my BRs (Brother-Rats) said, "Is it true?" I looked at her, perplexed at what she had asked.

"Shut your suck Rats!" One of the cadre asked me if I thought I could talk.

No sir, I thought to myself, *I didn't say anything,* as I briskly walked out to form up.

This was the longest march back to barracks because I knew what was coming. Once we fell out, I strained back to my room, and right behind me was my BR. Once in the room she asked, "Are you gay? Is it true?"

I replied, "Who told you that?"

She answered, "I heard from a friend."

I reluctantly stated, "Yes, but no one is supposed to know." At this point, I realized that people were going to find out, and the best I could hope for was to control the rate of speed it was spreading by asking people to not say anything. As the day went on and the rumors were swirling, I found myself in this place of not knowing what to do.

As people asked me the dreadful question, "Are you gay?" I would reply, "Yes, I am gay." Each time I said it out loud, I attempted to project confidence, but on the inside, I was sick to my stomach, and I was scared. Eventually, I told my roommates because I wanted them to hear it from me. Nothing changed between us, and one roommate said, "I don't care. Just don't try anything on me," as we all laughed. It only took one day for almost the entire Corps to find out.

There were a couple of social issues that were being dealt with during this time. There were those who thought that women shouldn't be at VMI. There were concerns about racism. But there wasn't anything worse than being gay. I was considered by some to be the lowest of the low, even though, being a Rat, I didn't think one could get any lower; but, I had reached rock bottom.

My intent in coming out was not to be the headline, yet there I was. The next night, I sat down with my Dyke, and I fully expected him to switch me out with someone else, try to give me up or ban me from the room. He did none of those things, and when I felt like most of the Corps was against me, he and my Uncle-Dykes (his roommates) stuck by my side.

I got the typical questions like, how do you know? When did you know? I welcomed these questions, though. I would answer them to the best of my ability. With each statement of being gay that I made, my confidence grew even more. Inside I still hadn't fully embraced and didn't really understand my sexuality. It wasn't lost on me that the questions being asked were for the purpose of understanding the situation better.

The Truth Will Set You Free

Coming out as being gay made VMI ten times harder, but I knew that I needed to tell Robert and Sarah about my coming to terms with my sexuality. Up to this point, there were some BR's and cadets who I thought would freak out at learning that I was gay, but they shrugged it off. So, I thought maybe I would have the same response from Robert and Sarah. I didn't have the fortitude to talk to Robert and Sarah over the phone or in person about being gay. Knowing how both felt about homosexuality based on religious and moral beliefs, I knew they would need a cooling down period.

I decided to sit down and write a letter which revealed that I was gay but pointed out nothing had changed. I explained that I wanted them to accept me for who I truly was. In writing the letter, I felt that I was giving them time to read it, time to think about it, and then time to respond.

One of the concerns that I had was that sometimes during moments of anger your mouth may say something that you don't really mean. Not only that, but once you say it, you can't take it back. I waited about a week after I sent the letter, and since I had heard nothing from Robert and Sarah, I called. As I spoke with Robert, he expressed how hurt and upset he was. He felt like they had been lied to the entire time that I lived with them. He told me that I was no longer a part of the family. He said that what I was doing was a sin and that I needed to get myself right with God. We just went around and around in the conversation.

Out of all the things in my life that I had experienced, I think this broke me down the most. I think it's because one of the things that I feared would happen had happened, and when it did, it was a surreal experience for me, and I wasn't fully prepared to handle it.

As I was starting on the journey to becoming comfortable in my own skin, I had lost my family. As I look back, I think some of the conversations I initially had with Robert were nails in the coffin of our relationship. They were the buildup towards the breakdown because each time something was said that was derogatory or demeaning, it separated us more and more.

I was aware that I would not have been at VMI had it not been for Robert and Sarah, and for this reason, I committed to keeping the door open in our relationship, regardless of what was said or done.

I felt there were many reasons why Robert and Sarah disowned me. Part of it was because of their religious beliefs, and part of it I felt I must take some ownership of. When I first came out as gay, I felt as though Robert and Sarah had to accept me for who I was in that moment. What I failed to realize was that what took me years to come to terms with wouldn't happen overnight or in a week with Robert and Sarah.

When I wrote the letter to them, I put them in a predicament as well because I demanded their acceptance and love. It was like being born again when the light switched on, and I expected everyone to be where I was in the current moment. I wanted to feel loved. I wanted to feel respected. I wanted to be embraced.

As I sat alone for a while after the phone conversation with Robert, I thought about my current situation as I leaned forward with my elbows on my legs and my face in my hands. It felt as though most people in the Corps hated me, and now my family had turned their backs on me too.

Silence, fear, and the all-too-familiar feeling of being alone resurfaced. It was interesting because, though there were faculty members and members of the Corps that supported me, the negative people's actions and words drowned out those that were positive. As I stood and started walking back towards the barracks, I told myself, *you will not cry, just make it to your room.*

As I got into barracks, I started to strain, I made it past the second stoop, and the coast was clear! On the third stoop, the coast was clear, or so I thought. As my foot hit the first step to get to the fourth stoop I heard, "Rat, stop!" *No, No, No.* I turned around to see a third-classman was coming from the shower. He stood in front of me and stared at me, but he didn't say a word. He then said, "As you were." I thought to myself, *that was weird, as I briskly walked to my room.*

Once in my room, I grabbed my blanket and curled up under my desk. Since it was too early to put my rack down, it was the only option I had. I laid there and realized that giving up was not an option. I was determined to make VMI work. It was now all I had left standing between me and going back to the place where I was born.

Over the next couple of days, I was exhausted mentally, but I kept smiling, and I learned many life lessons through this storm. It was during this time that I realized I had to learn to love myself and respect myself before I expected anyone else to. In all honesty, I don't even think that I liked myself at this point. How could I expect anyone else to understand me when I didn't understand myself?

I recognized that most people spend a lifetime trying to please others, and lose their identity attempting to meet others expectations of who they should be. In the end, they fail to recognize that their strength and their beauty is in knowing who they are and being comfortable in their own skin.

Life was a bit lonely at times for a while, but in the quiet times, I found that I learned more and more about myself. A short while after the disastrous coming out saga with Robert, I came out to my biological mom (Lenora) over the phone. I had kept in contact with her sporadically via phone, and as we spoke I said, "I have something to tell you."

She said, "Go ahead."

My voice started to quiver, and I said, "I think I'm gay Mom."

As I started to cry- she responded, "That's okay. It's just a phase, but I love you anyway." At first, I wanted to correct her on the "it's just a phase" thing, but I remained silent and saw the moment for what it truly was.

When the world had made it known that I wasn't good enough, my mother was there. She said, "I love you. You're my baby, and nothing is ever going to change that." This was the acceptance I needed and the push to keep moving. I don't think my mother ever really comprehended how that moment, which was seemingly small and insignificant to her, was a huge milestone for me.

As time passed, I learned ways to avoid issues and altercations. One evening, while I showered in Cocke Hall, which is a gymnasium outside of barracks, two upperclassmen walked into the showers and started hitting me with towels, taunting me and making homophobic slurs. I lost my temper and punched the guy that was closest to me, at which point his buddy jumped between us and broke up the altercation.

I had chosen to shower at this location out of respect for my male Brother-Rats, and to have some peace of mind that all would be comfortable. Before I had time to process what had happened, I was sitting in front of the commandant, and he asked if I planned on commissioning. I replied, "Yes sir."

He said, "Your sexuality or sexual preference is none of my concern, but if you have an issue, you will come and see me. We don't fight here." I appreciated the way he handled it because I did not know which way it was going to go. I just wanted to be given the opportunity to get my education and have a successful career in the military.

After this happened, there were times when I would be standing in formation or straining in barracks while going up the stairs, and I would hear, "Faggot Rat," "Fudge packer," and "dick sucker." How do you deal with that? I learned that you don't. I just ignored it and kept moving forward. In this environment, I knew the formula for change had to be done in a subtle way. I knew if I could affect the heart, the mind would follow.

By not responding, not feeding into the hatred, and continuing to have a positive outlook, I was changing the direction of the ship ever so slowly. Regardless of my frustration level, I continued to engage with those who didn't like me, and I helped those who wouldn't have helped me. Sometimes I look back over my life and thank God for allowing me to see the vision and have clarity when many of the negative events took place. I just kept reminding myself that it wasn't about me. Everything I had to endure was for the LGBT cadet who would come after me.

If my institutional knowledge is correct, I was the first openly gay cadet to come out while in the Rat-Line at VMI. Does it really matter? No. What it should say to future cadets is, if I could do it, then so can they. There were some tough times, but what I learned prepared me for life and what was to come after VMI.

There were times when I would literally hold my Brother-Rats or upperclassmen who would struggle with coming to terms with being gay. They would cry because they thought it was a curse and they didn't want to be like that. They would wonder how they would make it and how they could be successful.

Many fellow cadets dealt with pretending to be straight and dating females because they didn't want anybody to figure out their secret. As I helped some navigate these issues, it was apparent to me that I had a purpose. Many times, when negative things happen, people ask the question, "Why?" For me, for most of my life, when negative situations occurred, it was revealed to me within a short period of time why those things happened.

What being gay and out at VMI meant was that it gave other cadets who were gay the opportunity to see who supported me and who didn't. It opened the door for me to meet faculty members who were gay or supported LGBTQIA+ rights. It helped me meet alumni from both VMI and other schools like the Citadel, our rival, who were also gay. We became this tight knit-group. A whole new world emerged and became a part of my world. I began to heal.

What my being out, and eventually being proud about who I was led to, was other people who were gay or bi-curious opening up to me about their experiences. It has always helped me to help others. I also learned that at a small place like VMI, if I broke someone's trust, then no one else would trust me. When people let me in on their deepest, darkest secrets, whether it was their sexuality or significant trauma they had experienced, my response was always the same: This is the judgement-free zone, and what can I do to help?

What Does This Mean?

Initially, I didn't really know what being a gay man was all about. I didn't know what the culture was, though I had come out as gay. As a Rat, when it spread that I was gay, I had an upperclassman that kicked in my door, and as my roommates and I strained, he called me out on the stoop and asked, "Are the rumors true? Are you gay?"

I said, "Yes," and he said, "Okay. Me too," and he sent me back into my room. He wasn't out, but over the next year I would learn many lessons from him on what being gay meant in a military institute and outside of it.

Everyone in the Corps knew who I was even though I didn't know them. I quickly realized during my third-class year that I wasn't alone. I had become the face of the LGBTQIA+ community at VMI.

Whatever I did or didn't do was going to serve as the representation of what homosexuals were like. That was never my intention. It was a lot of weight to bear. I had to think about my actions and how I portrayed myself. I had to constantly monitor the pulse of the Corps in response to what I was doing because I didn't want to push too hard and ruin it for others.

I must admit that Terri B. had a huge impact on how I navigated this path. There were times when I wanted to do something crazy, like dress in drag. I would have to ask if people would find it funny or if it would be seen in a different light. She was constantly giving me advice on these things.

As I continued on my journey of learning what it meant to be gay, I went to my first gay club. It was called The Park was located in Roanoke, VA. I snuck off post, borrowed an upper-classman's car and went.

As I walked into the bar, I was anxious but excited. This tall, flamboyant, white male in his late 30's to early 40's walked up to me. I'd gotten there way too early. He said, "Hey girl, welcome to The Park. I haven't seen you around." I was thinking, *I don't know you. Why are you talking to me?* I was in defensive mode. I didn't know what to expect.

I put out my hand for him to shake and he said, "Oh no," and he hugged me. He tried to kiss me, and I pulled back. I thought, *I don't know where your lips have been, but I know they're not going on my face. I don't know you like that.* He looked at me as if to say, "Are you ok?" I wondered, *Is this normal? Is this what gay men do? Do they just walk up and kiss each other? What?*

It's so funny because I had "newbie" written all over me as I walked into the bar. I was already closed off if I didn't know a person. I was just learning and quickly realized that there is no single standard for being gay. There are no requirements. You don't have to talk, walk, or act a certain way.

Role Models

Eventually, I was introduced to Hank Thomas, a VMI alumnus, and his partner, Kevin Litschgi. Hank had retired from the Marine Corps as a Lieutenant Colonel and worked for the U.S. Department of Energy.

Meeting this couple while at VMI was one of the most important cornerstones of my becoming comfortable and confident. I was in my sophomore year when I met them. Because my previous introduction in high school to the nurse's friend wasn't the best, I was apprehensive at first. It took very little time to realize that Hank and Kevin were sincere and had the best intentions.

Through conversations, I learned that Hank had done it all. I tried to glean as much information from both Hank and Kevin as possible. Hank was a Christian who had been married, had kids and led an accomplished career in the military and the government. I knew that I could learn so much if I just listened. His goal was to make sure that I, and other LGBT cadets, had a safe place to go. Hank and Kevin opened their homes in Silver Spring, MD and Rehoboth, DE to me.

Overtime, not only did I become confident in who I was as a person, but I had created another family. It's so easy to focus on the negative things that are happening around you that you lose sight of the positive things. Neither Hank nor Kevin would allow me to lose my way, though.

Whenever I needed a place to go for holidays, or if I needed money, no questions were asked--I had it. Hank loved to talk about politics and history. Kevin was the complete opposite. He loved to have tea time while wearing flamboyant hats. He also loved to throw extravagant parties, dress up for Halloween, and travel on elegant cruise ships.

On one hand, you had Hank, who was stern and serious, but could lighten up and have fun. On the other hand, you had Kevin, who was the life of the party. These two people who were opposites in personality demonstrated that I too could be myself and be successful. I could have it all.

I was also fortunate enough to gain another mentor who graduated from the Citadel, Kevin, and his husband, Todd. Kevin and Todd were just as generous, loving, and opened their home as well. I learned that being gay wasn't going to be the curse that I had at one time thought it would be.

Finding God Again

You find faith quickly even if you don't have faith during the Rat-Line. For some, church is an excuse to get away from post. For others, it is truly an opportunity to worship.

One Sunday, we were all packed into Jackson Memorial Hall. Each pastor was given the opportunity to get up and speak about their church and invite Rats to join their church for worship services. As I sat and listened to each pastor speak, I was beginning to get discouraged because none of them said anything that resonated with me.

Then, Pastor G. stood up, and before he even spoke, his posture and presence moved me. I, along with several of my Brother-Rats, chose to go to Marlbrook Baptist Church, and off we went. It was like a breath of fresh air to be leaving post for a couple of hours.

While at church, I was fed both spiritually and literally. I was given the time to reflect on how far I had come. After church service, I ate and then I was given the opportunity to pick a host family.

The host family is a family that opens their home to a cadet and gives him/her a place to decompress. Interestingly, this was all happening while I dealt with coming to terms with being gay and having lost Robert and Sarah. I say "Lost" because although I knew exactly where they were, I didn't know exactly how I was going to repair the relationship.

After my initial phone conversation with Robert about being gay, I didn't want anything to do with church or God. I had to blame someone or something for what had happened, so I pointed my finger at God.

On this winding road called life it's interesting how fate pulled me back on course, even when I was determined to divert. The environment was such at VMI that I would have done anything to get away, just for a moment, to relax and clear my head.

I found myself sitting in a pew at Marlbrook Baptist Church. In a church, a place where I had sworn never to return, I sat there. Pastor G. said, "Love the person, regardless of the sin." I felt as though he spoke directly to my situation. Even though one might mention that it's Southwest Virginia, in a little rural town, that is conservative and traditional, the church stood on the word, but spoke through a filter of love.

As I was building a relationship with the church and the congregation, I ended up choosing the host family of Debbie and Scott S. They were an incredible family! They opened their home to me. They fed me. Like a recurring pattern, I was amazed at how every step of the way, God had placed people in my life that would pick up the torch to mentor me and help me to realize my potential.

Scott and Debbie lived on a farm that had horses and a kennel where they took care of dogs. One day, Scott was feeding the horses, and he took me down to the barn with him. As we walked into the stall, I was nervous about being so close without a barrier for protection. As Scott tended to the horses, he assured and reassured me the horses weren't going to hurt me.

A short time into this ordeal, I began to get comfortable with rubbing the horses' noses. Scott must have forgotten about me being uneasy and walked out of the stall and started to close the door behind him. I almost fainted, and when he realized what he had done, he came back into the stall and we erupted into laughter.

These are genuine, down-to-earth people. They wanted nothing but for me to be comfortable in their home and feel like I was at home.

Over time, we built a strong bond. They allowed me to stay with them during the summer for summer school and didn't charge me for any expenses. Each morning, Debbie would get up and drive me to school and then pick me up. She'd also fix dinner every night. It was truly a blessing how it all worked out. I felt like I didn't deserve the kindness that was shown to me at this time. I thought, *how am I ever going to pay them back?* Both Debbie and Scott told me not to worry about paying them back but to just pay it forward.

<u>Blessings from Above</u>

I struggled financially and had difficulty paying tuition, buying books, and supplies. To make money, I worked in the Career Services Department on campus. This was my first job, and I contacted alumni, organized charts, and completed office work. It was a good foundation to build from.

Another blessing that helped me continue at VMI was the Meredith Family Scholarship. The Meredith family provided me with a scholarship that helped me stay enrolled at VMI. I am forever grateful to the family for their generosity. As I teetered on the line due to poor academic performance, I was also teetering because of financial issues. I still don't know to this day how I was awarded this scholarship with everything going on, but I was.

As a recipient of the Meredith Family Scholarship, I would get together with the Merediths once or twice a year for a scholarship dinner. I'll never forget the first time I sat down at the table for a scholarship dinner.

I walked in and met the family, who were warm, kind-hearted, and easygoing. As we entered the restaurant, I immediately realized I was out of my element. There was too much silverware and fine china on the table. As if that wasn't enough, the menu had words I couldn't even pronounce. *Oh, fix it Jesus!* As I sat at the table and smiled, on the inside, I was thinking, *Jesus, please have something with chicken.*

I watched what everyone else did and which utensil they used, while I answered various questions about school. As I glanced at the menu, I saw menu items like duck à l'orange, frog legs, and escargot. I thought to myself, *there are many things that I am open-minded about trying, but food is not one of them. I prefer to keep my palate in the closet, if you will.* I laugh now because it was a learning moment. I eventually found a chicken entree and managed to not make a fool out of myself.

Becoming a Soldier

I'd taken out grants, loans, and obtained a scholarship, but it still wasn't enough. I realized that if I joined the Army National Guard, they would pay for school and I'd also have money. Initially, I was a Marine ROTC option. To be consistent, I joined the Army ROTC option.

I had two fears once I came to terms with my sexuality and knowing what my goals in life were. One was the possibility of being discharged from the military due to the Don't Ask, Don't Tell policy. The other was being discharged from the Officer Program for taking Adderall due to being diagnosed with ADHD (attention deficit hyperactivity disorder). I did not want these situations to prevent me from commissioning. There was nothing I could do about my sexuality, but I was determined to manage my ADHD without medicine. The question I had to ask and answer for myself was, *how bad did I want it?* If it is important to you, you will find a way. If not, you will find an excuse.

Joining the Army National Guard was a unique experience for me because being exposed to the Rat-Line meant I was overly prepared for basic training. I went through OSUT infantry school at Fort Benning. I attended with several VMI cadets who were in similar financial situations.

Somehow, in a short period of being at basic training, my being gay came to the surface. The unit I was assigned to knew about my sexuality, and no one outwardly had an issue with it. I learned that each new environment meant I would have to experience the coming-out process all over again, though.

I felt like the focus should have been on training, and that it really wasn't the place, or time, to have to worry about it. What I also learned is that I didn't get to set the time or place to have these conversations. I would have to set aside my frustration and rise to the occasion.

Like each time before, I had to deal with the comments and the attitudes. It became clear to me that VMI had set the foundation for how to handle these challenges.

It was summer in Georgia, and I, along with my basic training class, was rushed off the bus by drill sergeants who yelled and ordered us to stand at attention in front of the barracks. As we stood in the sweltering heat, we were organized by company and then platoon. This was the first day, and I could only imagine what was about to happen.

All the drill sergeants then lined up with scowls on their faces. It was almost as if they were staring straight through my soul. In my mind I thought, *Lord, not this craziness again*. A speech was given, and then we got to meet our cadre. This had just become a game for me, albeit a familiar game.

We were all worked out, and then just as quickly as the chaos began, it stopped, and we were all led into the barracks. While some appeared to be thinking, "OMG (oh my god) what did I get myself into," I thought it was hilariously funny, as did the other cadets I attended with. They also recognized, as did I, that we had a responsibility to help our squad mates with the knowledge we had gained from VMI.

In the barracks, there were rows of bunk beds with foot lockers at the end of them and wall lockers beside them. In the middle of the floor that ran almost the entire length of the barracks, was a design that was outlined with a black line. "Toes on the line and stand at attention," was the direction given by the senior drill sergeant. "If I call out something that applies to you, sound off and we are going to give you a colored piece of tape so that you can be recognized."

Collectively we all yelled "Yes, drill sergeant."

"Cold weather injuries"— A recruit standing to my left sounded off. "Hot weather injuries," —The same recruit sounded off again. "Allergic to bees"— You guessed it, the same recruit sounded off.

The drill sergeant walked towards him and said, "Are you shitting me. You're the fucking rainbow!" We all snickered and the push-ups began. It was apparent the recruit was scared and didn't want to be there by the tone in his voice. The shark attack had shocked this recruit.

After an exhausting day of expectations, learning about the assault rifle, and PT (physical training), I was exhausted and ready for sleep. Finally, the yelling had ceased and we were all given permission to go to bed.

As I dozed off, the recruit that had clearly struggled throughout the day to learn the basics of being a soldier, got up to use the bathroom. While in the bathroom, the recruit attempted to cut his wrist with a shaving razor. He was found by his battle buddy crouched in the corner as he cried.

The drill sergeants were notified, and he was removed for a short period of time. When he returned, the recruit was adamant about getting out of the military. No matter how much the squad attempted to talk him down, he was determined to find a way out.

One afternoon, as we all cleaned the barracks and buffed the floor, we were sure we were ready for an inspection. We took advantage of the downtime to get to know one another. When no one paid attention, the recruit took the cord of the buffer, wrapped it around his neck, and flipped the machine over the window sill. No one could get to him fast enough, and then I heard the crash. As everyone froze, I heard boots coming up the stairs at a quick pace, and the drill sergeants busted through the door. There the recruit stood staring at the squad and the squad staring at him.

The Senior Drill Sergeant yelled, "You're shitting me! You have failed. For crying out loud, you can't even kill yourself right." The recruit, as he cried, yelled something that was inaudible and then I heard, "I want to go home." The other drill sergeants took the cord from around his neck and he was whisked away.

A short while later, all three drill sergeants were standing in our barracks, and we were asked if anyone else wanted to kill themselves. The room was silent. "Now that we've got that bull shit out of the way, is my barracks ready?"

We all replied in unison, "Yes, drill sergeant." As the inspection began, it became clear that we had missed all kinds of things and thus a tornado spontaneously formed, and mattresses, blankets, and foot lockers were whirled around the barracks. We obviously weren't ready.

The Senior Drill Sergeant walked out, followed by the other two. Before he left, he said, "It better be spotless when I return." His statement set panic in some because we weren't given a time frame.

I didn't really care. We could only do it as fast as we could. While some were mad, I laughed, which only made things worse. I explained that my mother had done this to me as a child and it wasn't anything new.

We truly had amazing drill sergeants. Though they said and approached things in a different manner than I would have, I could clearly see through the harsh statements and bravado.

It was in the Senior Drill Sergeant's eyes. He was shaken at the thought of losing one of his recruits. While some could only focus on the words, I looked deeper into that moment. The process had worked. This was the first of three that would go.

Shortly after this incident, another recruit who was ordered by the court to join, made it clear he wasn't going to tolerate being disrespected or yelled at. I was shocked that a judge could and/or would do such a thing.

As we stood in formation at attention preparing for a movement, I heard, "Stop looking at me like that." *Hold up, that wasn't a drill sergeant! That was a recruit!* In my head, I clutched my pearls, and wanted to look so badly, but knew my drill sergeants had eyes in the back of their heads, so I maintained discipline.

I can't recall exactly what occurred, but the recruit swung at the drill sergeant. Listen, *to hell with discipline at that moment*. Everyone broke attention and stared as drill sergeants descended upon the recruit.

Like sharks that could smell blood in the water from miles away, they came. Like the animals going into the ark two by two, they came. My mind couldn't make sense of what my eyes had seen.

The recruit eventually realized he wasn't going to win and was overpowered. While pinned to the ground, he yelled at the drill sergeant, "I stole on your punk ass." He was subdued and whisked away.

The funniest thing happened after this incident. Have you ever been at a place where a kid acts up and other parents chastise their children even though they didn't do anything wrong? We were told to toe the line, which meant to go back into the barracks. Our Senior Drill Sergeant came in and said, "Anyone want to try that bullshit? I promise you won't get the best of me."

"Half right face!" I thought, *are you kidding me? We didn't do anything wrong*. We were pushed until muscle failure.

The lesson taught was that even though it wasn't our platoon, if you are part of an organization, your actions affect the entire organization.

One of the things I enjoyed during training was the ruck marches. A ruck march is a relatively fast march over various distances while carrying a load. As training progressed, the marches got longer and longer.

There was one recruit who was small in stature. I would say, if I had to guess, he was 5'5". He had a hard time when it came to ruck marches and the heat. Often, we all would pitch in to help carry his ruck or his weapon. On our final ruck march, even before we started, it was clear he wasn't in the right mindset.

He had just dealt with blisters that had all but healed from the last ruck march. Being smaller meant he had to work twice as hard to keep up. I admired him for his drive, and even though he needed help, he kept pushing.

This time it was different. At about 12 miles in, the recruit had given his ruck up and was barely holding his assault weapon. As if he was drunk, he walked in almost a diagonal from the middle of the road, to the outside of the road, and then back again.

A mile later, his weapon was gone and he was still struggling. All of the drill sergeants were feared by most, but the First Sergeant was unmatched in his experience and wisdom. Here was a man who had done it all, and his very presence spoke volumes.

As he came up on my left, not even breaking a sweat, I heard him clear his throat, and I saw him direct his gaze at the recruit. "What the hell is this shit?" The Senior Drill Sergeant was now coming up as well, and I could tell he was embarrassed. We were all halted.

The First Sergeant yelled, and Senior Drill Sergeants repeated, "Hydrate," and in response the recruits yelled, "Or die." We sat down, and some pulled their boots off to tend to their blisters, while others took their rucks off to relieve the pain in their shoulders or back.

The First Sergeant walked up to the recruit and said, "You will finish this march, and you will do it with all of your gear." As he walked away the Senior Drill Sergeant came over. I was both excited and anxious to hear what was going to come out of his mouth. I found his dry sense of humor and quick wit to be hilarious and refreshing.

The Senior Drill Sergeant was standing over the recruit, and he had a sneer of disgust on his face. I bit my tongue because just his look was enough for me to start laughing.

He said, "Recruit, your battle buddy is about five miles down this road and if you don't get to him he's going to die; dig deep. Your fellow recruits have carried you long enough."

I was now staring at the Senior Drill Sergeant like, *are you kidding me? Way to let me down on this one.* I guess the expression on my face said the same thing because he snapped his head towards me and snarled, "Shut up, Diggs!" and walked away.

All of us around the recruit, including myself, did what we could to motivate him, and some of us even took a few items out of his ruck. As we got up and started again, almost immediately, the recruit started falling back, and I decided that I would stay with him.

As others passed us, I told him just to keep moving forward and put one foot in front of the other. The recruit started saying, "I can't do it."

My response was, "You've made it this far. Fight. You can't give up now."

The recruit replied, "My legs hurt. My feet hurt."

My response was, "Stop focusing on the pain and keep moving." I also told the recruit to stop walking in a diagonal movement. I explained that in doing so he was using more energy, but my words were futile.

As we approached the outside of the road, without warning, the recruit threw himself in the ditch. As he landed, his ruck was underneath him and he looked like a turtle stuck upside down with his feet flailing in the air.

"Move along Diggs," I heard from the First Sergeant who had hung back as well. As I began moving, I could hear the Senior Drill Sergeant and the First Sergeant yelling at the recruit to get up, but he refused. As I finished the ruck march, I was both bothered and amused by what had occurred. I will never forget the sight of the recruit on his back with his legs kicking in the air. Sometimes in the darkest of situations, humor will pull you through.

"Formation"

At infantry school, I felt like I had to push myself harder than others to prove I belonged or that I was just as valuable. Being at infantry school, and being gay, was an issue, but being black and gay in that environment was a whole other issue. this was too much to bear for some.

I was constantly fighting negative stereotypes and people's perceptions. One incident that set the standard for what I would and would not tolerate was during a movement exercise. My squad was moving through the woods.

For this iteration, I was selected as the squad leader, which meant that I maneuvered the squad in combat. Gary, the rear team leader, was upset because he felt like we should have used bounding overwatch. I also believed at the time he was upset because I didn't put him as the front team leader.

I acknowledged his opinion and continued using traveling overwatch, which are two different squad movement techniques.

Gary, an Asian male who towered over most of our basic class with a solid build, was arrogant, and in my opinion, took things too seriously at times. He was the type that had to have the perfect score in everything and when placed in a leadership role, drove those under his charge crazy. As usual, it came back to me being black and gay.

"Listen, you fucking, nigger faggot! You're going to get us all killed!"

As everyone started laughing, I looked at him and replied, "Your mom should have been killed for having you." In my head I was thinking to myself, *has he lost his mind? This is all pretend and we are shooting blanks in these scenarios.*

All of sudden, I felt dizzy and things started spinning. I realized that he had hit me. I couldn't believe he had punched me. I spun around, charged him, lifted him up and slammed him, mounted him, and punched him in his ribs repeatedly until some of the squad mates pulled me off him.

Afterwards, I kept saying that my head hurt badly. One of the guys said, "He hit you in the head with an e-tool dude!" This is also known as an entrenching tool and is a collapsible spade. I don't know how it didn't break the skin. My head felt like it had been run over by a car.

When I realized he had hit me with the e-tool, and I saw it on the ground as they separated us, I had this burning desire to really hurt him. I felt like I had gone easy on him during the fight. I went after him again but I didn't get to him. For the most part, any time I had gotten into any kind of altercation, I usually regretted it at the end. I would think, *how did I allow someone to push me to act out of character?* For when you allow someone to control your emotions, you have given them the power to control you.

This time, I wasn't bothered. Gary was one of the few that always had something to say about me being weaker because I'm gay, so he had it coming. After that incident, I earned his respect. I would have thought that being a motivator, going back and helping those that were struggling, understanding and knowing movements and the different weapon systems, would have impressed him and would have brought him around.

In that moment, the only thing that earned his respect was me beating the crap out of him after he hit me in the head with an e-tool. This situation taught me that some people don't respect others until they are checked and sometimes you don't get to choose how it will play out. I don't advocate violence. I try to always find a way to circumvent it. In this, I lived on and he lived with a little bit of embarrassment.

Recruits would pick on him because he got beat up by a gay guy and they would say to him, "How did you lose the fight after you hit him with an e-tool? That doesn't make any sense."

My First Loss

It was a typical Georgia day, hot and humid. My squad and I were practicing movements across open fields while under attack. I looked across the field and the Captain and First Sergeant were approaching. This was rare and we all knew immediately that something wrong.

As they got closer, the Senior Drill Sergeant was called over just outside of hearing range. We were all nervous and as we stood in a circle, recruits started telling on themselves. I looked at them and thought, *you all break way too easy,* and then I heard the First Sergeant yell, "Diggs, front and center." I ran over and snapped to attention. As I ran towards them, I thought to myself, *what could I have done wrong?*

The Senior Drill Sergeant gathered the squad and he took them away. The Captain said, "I regret to inform you that your grandmother has passed away." I heard him, but he couldn't have said what I thought he said. The Captain repeated himself and I was overtaken by emotion.

As my knees hit the ground I thought, *What? How? Why, this can't be.* I couldn't remember the entire exchange of words from the Captain and the First Sergeant, but I was told that I would be granted emergency leave.

As I buried my face into my hands, the First Sergeant walked over to me and said, "You are one of the strongest recruits I've seen come through training. You get up, you be strong, and you honor her memory." His words touched me in a way that I couldn't describe.

When my grandmother Ruth Waters was diagnosed with cancer, I made sure that I got to spend time with her every time an opportunity presented itself. Each moment that I spent with her I treated as if it were our last. So, before I had left to go to infantry school, I made sure to tell her how much I loved her.

My issue was that I didn't get to say goodbye. I wasn't there when it was her time to rest and that in my head I thought she had more time to live. I left basic training and went back home for the funeral. I stood before family and friends and sang, "His Eye is on the Sparrow," for her celebration of life.

At the moment I began to sing, and I felt the pain was too much to bear, I thought about the First Sergeant's words. Once my grandmother was laid to rest, I went back to training and successfully completed infantry school.

At the end of infantry school, my drill sergeants came to me and said, "We are giving you this opportunity. We want you to go on to get your wings."

I looked at them and said, "Thank you for the opportunity, but I'm not jumping out of a perfectly flying plane. That's not happening." In my head I thought, *I'll keep my feet on the ground. I'll shoot, move, and communicate. I'll do whatever I need to do on the ground, but I ain't jumpin' out of no plane.* My drill sergeants did not find me turning down the opportunity amusing and smoked me (worked me out).

Walking Tall

After experiencing infantry school, I was confident in who I was as a person. I would challenge people's perspectives in a respectful manner about a multitude of issues. These issues included; women attending VMI and the Battle Flag of Robert E. Lee commonly called the Confederate flag.

I would tell fellow cadets, "Sure there are women who don't belong here, but there are also men that don't belong here as well and yet you don't say anything. At least be consistent." There was a debate one time on if the Confederate flag was racist.

I could understand both sides of the issue, but to prove a point, I went and purchased a Confederate flag belt and some cowboy boots. I switched into civvies and wore the outfit to see what kind of response I would get.

There were those who laughed and told me I looked like a fool, while there were some that told me I didn't have a right to wear the belt. When pressed on why I shouldn't wear it, I was told because it's a southern pride thing. I would then mention that I was from North Carolina. I pressed them on what their point was.

For me, this was about getting people to look at things in a different light. It was about taking a moment and stepping away from emotion and seeing an issue from another person's perspective. You must have thick skin. Sometimes, I took the ignorance that some people displayed in the hopes that in the future they would recognize it, grow, and change. I realized that as a people, our perceptions and beliefs are based off what we are taught and exposed to.

Anything that challenges our norms or that is outside of the boundaries I term as "other." It's easier for some to hate, devalue, or dismiss others because they can be viewed as a threat, not normal, or less than. Once a person, whether by force, fate, or choice develops a relationship with that person or group, the ability to hold on to the previous-misconceptions wanes. That's what I experienced at VMI.

I learned how to wrestle and how to box. I would always go up against the biggest person because I had to make sure that people understood that even though I'm gay, it didn't mean that I was weak.

Going into VMI, I was familiar with pools and water, but I still wasn't a swimmer. While at VMI, I had to learn how to successfully complete combat swimming. You must be able to successfully combat swim to graduate from VMI. I also needed to do it to commission.

I was not interested in large pools of water, jumping into the water, or making your BDU (battle dress uniform) into a flotation device. I would jokingly mention, "That's not for me. That's white people stuff." The instructor and everyone present would laugh and I'd look puzzled as why they thought it was funny. It took a lot of time, patience and effort for me to meet the standards, but with lots of assistance from my colleagues and superiors, I did.

I've always had a fear of heights. There were some obstacle courses where I had to climb up ladders and jump off into the water. It took a lot of prodding, poking, and chanting to get me to complete the goal. I wasn't ashamed of letting everyone know that I had a fear of heights. When you added water, laugh all you want, but I was not going out like that.

I was very thankful for the cadre and my Brother-Rats who encouraged me until I was comfortable. I never had the personality where I had to be the baddest person in the room. All in all, as time went on multiple things were happening at once, I was constantly learning about myself. I was impacting people's perceptions and perspectives.

It was important for me to accept people where they were. Once the friendship was established I would challenge why he/she felt the way they did. I learned that you can agree to disagree and still be civil. You don't have to agree on every single point in order to work together to accomplish the mission.

Some of the cadets that had issues with my sexual orientation allowed me into their spaces while avoiding the conversation about the issue. I was told often, "I'm not gay and I don't think that being gay is right, but you're a pretty cool person."

Some wondered if, because I was gay, I would be attracted to all the men at VMI. I would state, "No. Are you attracted to all of the women who attend VMI or all of the women you meet?" Instead of yelling and arguing, I would ask questions.

If I choose to be gay, then when did you choose to be straight? If being gay is such a glorious lifestyle, then why do so many people hide it or commit suicide? The questions would often be met with silence. Looking back, at the time, I had so much support, yet I still felt all alone. It's tough to explain, but when you want someone (Robert/Sarah) to love you and you feel they don't, you lose sight of the many people who do.

As my cadetship continued, several of my fellow cadets and their parents provided me with either a place to stay, money, food, or all three at times. VMI was now my home and my Brother-Rats were my family.

As people would return to post after breaks during the year, some would get nervous or have a pit in their stomach because they dreaded returning. For me, call me crazy, but I couldn't wait to return to post.

"Lean Not to Your Own Understanding"

When I became eligible to sign my intent to commission, I chose to enlist with the Army Reserves. Though my initial plan, goal, and dream was to go active duty, the quiet inner voice that I had often found guiding me was pushing me in another direction.

I had learned at this point in my life that even when I didn't understand it, or the inner voice was going against what I wanted, I had to listen to it. I felt like I had so much to offer and all I wanted was an opportunity to perform well in my job.

As I sat and signed my contract with the recruiting operation officer, I stared at the paper for quite some time. I then paused, looked up and asked, "If I want to change this, can I?" I was told that I could. It wasn't that I didn't trust that I was doing the right thing, it was me trying to push back. I wanted to ensure that I had an out, leaving a way to the dream I wanted to fulfill.

I had just started my first relationship with a guy. I wanted to be proud because I found love, but I knew that my love wasn't accepted. In the end, one day, I may have had to choose between the military or living in authenticity.

"What's Love Got to Do With It?"

Dating in Lexington VA, was sparse to say the least. With so much going on in my life, it was almost impossible to do. I signed up for a couple of social networking sites which connected me to the world.

I met a guy named Tanner that I began chatting with frequently. Before I knew it, we had decided to meet for dinner and hangout for the weekend. I couldn't believe it! I was going on my first date! I wondered if he was going to look like his pictures, what he would sound like, and how he would be in person.

I admired that he decided to drive all the way from Kentucky to Lexington, VA. He was going to pay for a hotel for the weekend so we could hang out and see where things would go. I had never really worried about getting in trouble at VMI, but the week leading up to our date, I was extremely cautious to ensure sure nothing was going to prevent me from leaving post.

After I finished all my obligations on post, my feet couldn't move fast enough. I headed off downtown to meet him. As I neared the business where we were supposed to meet, I abruptly stopped because I had to check my uniform, do the breath test (the one where you cup your hand and blow into your own face,) and wiped the sweat off my face. I walked in the door and I could tell immediately who Tanner was. Not only because I had seen pictures, but he also had this look of surprise on his face.

I walked over to the table. He stood, gave me a hug and said, "You are hot. You look way better than your pictures." I glared at him and he said, "I mean that in a good way." His face turned red as we both laughed. To describe Tanner, he had a baseball player build, with a Kentuckian accent, amazing teeth, and a wonderful sense of humor. We talked and laughed until my jaws hurt. The date was refreshing and I had a blast. I didn't know what to expect, but I was pleasantly surprised.

As it got close to taps, I told Tanner that we'd have to catch back up on Saturday, because I didn't want to get boned for not being back in barracks. He laughed and asked, "What are you talking about?" I started blushing because I realized how what I said came across. This lead to me explaining that taps is played by a trumpet and when it sounds in barracks a cadet must be in an authorized location. If he/she is not, then they are bound by the honor code to report themselves. At which time, you could face a myriad of consequences.

Tanner looked at me and asked, "So you don't get to spend the night with me?" I looked at him and said, "Unfortunately not, but let's see about tomorrow night." We got up and he offered to take me back to post, which I appreciated, because at this point I would have had to run the entire way to make it on time. Once on post, he pulled over and said, "Thank you for an amazing time."

I replied, "The pleasure's all mine. I can't wait to see you tomorrow." He then looked at me and started to lean over as he closed his eyes. I backed my head up to the window and put the palm of my hand up to his face. "Ohh noo! Not in front of barracks! And oh by the way, I don't kiss on the first date."

I could tell he was a little embarrassed as he burst into laughter. In my head I thought, *you only get one chance to make a first impression.* As I said goodnight and got out of the car, I checked over my shoulder to make sure he was watching as I walked away, and he was. Yes!

I returned to my room and there was no sleep to be had. My mind raced with the endless possibilities. The next day, I decided to take the weekend, which meant I could stay the night at the hotel, if I wanted too.

That Saturday was the slowest day ever, it felt like I would never finish tasks and formations. Finally, the time came where I could meet with Tanner. We decided to explore Goshen and do a little bit of hiking.

At one point, we sat by the Maury River and just talked about life and our plans for the future. I decided I wanted to kiss him and as I closed my eyes and leaned in, I felt his hand on my face and burst out laughing as he said, "I don't kiss on the second date." As I laughed, he leaned in and kissed me and said, "Wow that's the first time I've ever kissed a guy in public."

I looked at him and said, "I bet you tell that to every guy you've kissed."

"No, I'm not out to my friends at home."

We then went to dinner, and as the night went on he said, "I guess it's time to take you back to barracks."

"No, tonight taps is a little later. So what's next?"

"Everything seems to close early around here, and I know the hotel isn't appropriate. I don't know."

"Well, if I'm spending the night with you, then I guess it is appropriate."

He looked at me with a big smile and said, "Are you serious?"

"Yes," I replied.

As we drove to the hotel, I didn't say much, because I was wondering if this was going to be just a hookup or if it was going to become a relationship. I wanted our relationship to be clear but I also didn't want to seem overly impressed or desperate. I was still fighting an internal conflict about my self-image.

As we got to the hotel and walked in, Tanner caught the eye of the clerk. She waved him over to the front desk and asked him how his night was going. As I stood there in my cadet uniform, I thought, *what in the world is going on? Girl, stop.* I smirked as the clerk flirted, and I almost lost it when she asked, "How long are you going to stay in town?"

Tanner replied, "As long as he wants me to," and nodded in my direction. The clerk laughed, though I don't think she quite caught what he was trying to say. I started to get bored with the conversation and I was ready to hangout. Tanner, with his Southern charm, couldn't find a respectful way to break away from the conversation, so I went from being annoyed to being amused.

Eventually the clerk asked if he had a special someone in his life. He said, "I'm not sure yet." Before he could finish his sentence, the clerk piped up and said, "I don't have anyone."
Tanner replied, "Well, hopefully you will find someone. Goodnight."

As we walked to the elevator, I poked fun at Tanner for taking so long to let her down easy. He poked fun at me for not saving him. Once in the hotel room, I began to wonder if I was supposed to ask what we were or if it was too soon. I figured I'd just go with the flow, and see where things led.

"How do you sleep?" Tanner asked.

"On my side." I answered.

Tanner busted out laughing and said, "That's not what I meant. I looked at him, confused. He looked at me and said, "Night shorts, night pants, or nothing?

I replied, "Is a chastity belt an option?" His face turned red and we laughed.

As it came time for bed, we talked all night until I fell asleep. The next morning when I woke up, I thought to myself, *there is no way this guy is real. Something has to be wrong with him, but I'm going to see how long this lasts.* After we ate breakfast, I knew that Tanner had to head home because he had quite the drive back to Kentucky. I dreaded the moment.

As we finished up, and he took me back to barracks, I was crushed. *Will he call? Did I do and say the right things? Is he going to think I'm a prude?* As we stopped in front of Washington Arch, Tanner said, "Hopefully you had a good time."

"It was alright, I guess." I said sarcastically.

"Best damn time you'll ever have." He replied with a smirk.

I started laughing so hard because of his accent and the way he pronounced his words. The moment ended with a hug and Tanner telling me he would call me when he got home.

From the moment he left, I checked my cell phone for messages and waited, rather impatiently, for the phone to ring. Finally, almost six hours later, the phone rang and it was Tanner telling me that he was at home. We spoke for quite a bit of time and finally he said, "I've been thinking about something and I don't know how to say it." I'm clutching my imaginary pearls. I just know he's about to ask if we can date. "Would you... ahh, would you like to..." *Oh my God, spit it out!*

"Yes!" I exclaimed. I was so excited that I responded before he finished the question.

He started to laugh and asked, "When's your next break? Uhmm... Spring Break. Good. I'll pick you up and bring you home to meet my family."

Hold up, *was that what he was going to ask?* I was embarrassed because I realized by the tone of his voice that I jumped the gun. Just to be sure I asked, "Am I meeting your family as a friend?"

"Yeah, if that's okay with you."

"Yeah," I responded, trying to sound excited. Our friendship grew over time and we spent a lot of time talking and really getting to know each other. Then the day came for him to pick me up. I was so excited that I could barely control myself. I'd rehearsed how I would respond when he arrived. I would walk out, unbothered, put my bags in the trunk, and play it cool.

Well, it didn't work the way I'd planned. As I walked out, I tried to be nonchalant, but I tripped and looked like a baby gazelle just learning how to walk. As I recovered, cadets and Tanner were laughing at me. I just wanted to get in the car and drive away. Once in the car, Tanner told me that when we got into town, before going to his parents' home, we were going to meet his family for dinner. I thought to myself, *we have several hours on the road, and by the time we get there I'm just going to want to go to sleep.* I asked, "Can't we do it tomorrow?

He replied, "I don't want it to be awkward, so I asked the family to dinner."

"Cool, I get it." As we had done before, we spoke about all kinds of things during our trip and the time in the car flew by.

Before you knew it, we were pulling up to the restaurant. I was meeting his mother, father, and his two siblings. As we got out of the car, Tanner asked me if I was nervous. I looked at him with a confused expression because I didn't understand why I would be nervous. We were just friends and I was meeting his family.

"I'm good."

We entered the restaurant and we walked through two dining areas to a side banquet room. Tanner entered the room first and I followed. Immediately, when I walked into the room the looks on his family's faces told me I should be nervous.

It was as if the blood had drained from his parents' faces. His sister had a shocked expression on her face, and his brother had a smirk that read 'this is going to be good'. You could cut the tension in the room with a knife. There I stood wondering if I should back out of the room and leave, while trying to figure out what I had missed.

Tanner attempted to hug his mother and she brushed him off. He tapped his dad on the shoulder and then sat across the table in front of him. I greeted his brother first. I shook his hand. His sister just said, "Hi." I then spoke to both of his parents who barely acknowledged me.

As I sat down beside Tanner and across from his mother, Tanner's brother got up and switched sides. He was now sitting on the side with his parents. All I could think to myself, as I briefly stared at Tanner was, *what the hell did you get me into and why didn't you prepare me for this.*

The server came in and started to take drink orders. Even the Server appeared to pick up on the awkwardness. We sat there in silence as Tanner stared at the table. So, I broke the silence.

"Do you all come here often?"

Tanner's brother stated, "Usually on Sundays after church."

"What's good on the menu?"

Tanner's brother replied, "I don't know. Dad what do you think?"

"Everything is good," his dad responded. At this time, the server entered the room with our drinks.

Tanner went completely into shutdown mode. I was thankful for the server because at least I could have a normal conversation with her. I listened as everyone placed their orders and then I went last out of respect.

After the server left, Tanner's mom looked at me and asked, "Who are you and how do you know my son?" I started going into me being a cadet at VMI and having plans to go into the military. I skipped over the part of how we met. Tanner's mom looked at me and said, "I didn't catch your name."

"Deuntay, Ma'am."

She snapped, "Don't say Ma'am to me!" In my head I thought to myself, *lady I don't know you, but if you keep being nasty, it's going to be a problem.*

Finally, Tanner engaged, looked at his mom, and said, "Stop it."

We returned back to silence. Tanner and his father seemed to be having a stare off contest. When the food arrived, I was over the entire awkward situation. I just wanted to leave. Clearly, everyone was agitated, with the exception of Tanner's brother, everyone was just picking at their food.

"Who is this colored boy, Tanner?"

I clutched my "pearls" and choked on my spit. I looked around the room and thought, *'who is she referring to?'* I slid my chair back and started to stand up to leave. I knew if I started to act out and make a scene, it would have only confirmed whatever misperceptions his parents already had.

As I stood up, Tanner grabbed my hand and pulled down. In an elevated tone, he asked me to sit. I noticed that at this point he was still holding my hand as he looked across the table at his parents. Tanner then said, "I have something I need to share with y'all. I'm gay and this is my boyfriend." His family and I all stared at him like *what did you just say?*

Tanner's mother stormed out of the room as she said, "I can't believe you'd date a black guy." Tanner's sister got up and followed her mother. I was left with Tanner, his father, and his brother. Tanner's father, who had been mostly quiet the entire dinner, looked at Tanner as if I wasn't there and said, "You know how we feel about this. Why did you think that it would be okay to bring him here?"

My mind was racing as I tried to understand what just happened. *Tanner came out to his parents. His parents are okay with him being gay, but they don't like black people.* I looked at Tanner and I said, "I want to go back." I didn't have a car and I was at his mercy. I hated feeling like I was stuck.

Tanner looked at his dad and said, "If I have to take him back, then I won't ever come back here again." His dad got up and went to find his wife. Tanner's brother started to laugh and said, "You're going to kill 'em."

I thought to myself, *this is a nightmare. I'm going to wake up any moment now.* Tanner looked at me and started apologizing as tears begin to fall from his eyes. I was so overwhelmed by what had occurred that I had no compassion or empathy in the moment. The question that kept repeating in my head was, *why didn't he tell me*, and eventually I asked. Tanner replied, "I didn't plan for it to go this way. I'll see if we can stay at a friend's house and I'll take you back in the morning."

That night, we stayed with one of his friends. From the time we left the restaurant, to the time we got to his friend's house, we talked about what had happened. I wasn't interested in meeting anyone else, so we sat in the car down the street until Tanner's friend was in bed and then we went to the house.

Tanner's mother kept calling his phone but he refused to answer. He wouldn't tell me why his parents disliked black people, but he said it stemmed from a past issue. He told me his family needed more time to heal. Tanner began to tell me all the wonderful things about his family, and I half listened. I wasn't really interested in what he was saying after what I had witnessed.

I asked him why he didn't tell me that he wasn't out to his family and if he really had to come out the way he did that evening. Tanner looked at me and said, "I knew I wanted to date you when you didn't try to have sex with me in the hotel room. I thought it was too soon to say something. Most guys I have met are interested in me just for my looks. I guess it really doesn't matter at this point."

I replied, "Looks are temporary man. Life has taught me it's what's on the inside that counts." Tanner replied, "If you will give me a chance, I'll move to Virginia so we can be together."

I said, "Family is important. You shouldn't leave them behind. If your family can accept you for being gay, you are leagues beyond where some are. I'm exhausted. Let's finish this conversation in the morning."

When I woke up, Tanner was gone. As I wandered through the living room, I started to panic. I walked back to the room I had slept in and grabbed my phone and called him. He picked up on the first ring and said, "My buddy and I are on our way back with food and my family is on the way over. Before I take you back, my mother would like to apologize."

"I don't need an apology, but thanks," I replied. "I'll see you when you get back."

Call me crazy, but I think he waited down the street so that everyone would arrive at the same time. I stayed in the bedroom until Tanner walked in. At which point, he told me that his mom wanted to speak with me if it was okay. I thought to myself, *I'm not going to give her the luxury of making herself feel better.* But I decided that it did not make a difference at this point. He walked out of the bedroom and she walked in. As I sat on the bed, she motioned if it was okay to sit down on the bed as well. I nodded in approval.

His mother said, "I don't want to lose my first born. I don't always say or do the right things but if it will keep him here I apologize". I caught that it was not really an apology, but I said to myself, *alrighty, two can play this game.*

I jumped up and said I'm looking forward to getting to know you and as she stuck her hand out, I pushed it aside and gave her a big hug. I could feel her body tense up, and in that moment, I was determined to figure out where her hate was coming from.

I released her, and she left the room rather quickly, probably because she had to go wash off. Tanner came back in the room and asked if I would be willing to stay and I responded, "Yes." He then said the family had something fun planned just for me.

After getting ready, I went out into the living room to spend time with his family and to officially meet his friend. After everyone was done eating, it was time to head off on an adventure.

As we drove for a very long time, I noticed that we were going further and further into the wilderness. Before I knew it, we were traveling down a one lane road through the woods and going up the side of a mountain.

I thought to myself, as I smiled, *they are going to kill me out here*, as I looked down at my phone. I didn't have any signal and even if I did, I wouldn't have the slightest clue as to where I was. We got to a clearing and I realized where they had brought me. It was a family owned lot on the side of a mountain where they practiced shooting targets.

The family had as many guns as a regiment in the army would have. I thought to myself, *This is it. This is how it will end.* As the day went on, everyone dropped their guard, we laughed, and enjoyed each other's company. Before we left, Tanner told me we were staying at his parent's house and having dinner there as well. I just nodded in agreement. I thought to myself, *I'm on this horse. I might as well ride it at this point.*

As we descended from the side of the mountain, Tanner's friend kept staring at me. Finally, I asked, "What's up?"

He replied, "You don't look gay."

I said, "Well, what does gay look like?"

"I don't mean to be offensive but my childhood friend came out as gay this morning and neither of you look gay."

I explained that being gay had nothing to do with one's mannerisms or appearances.

As the week went on, I reverted to my 'kill them with kindness' mindset. It ended up paying off. The hardest one out of the family to get to open up was Tanner's grandmother. I must say she had a wealth of knowledge, and she didn't care about telling the family's secrets. She had a carefree mindset of who's going to check me.

I learned the hatred this family had, stemmed from Tanner's sister allegedly being raped by a black man. All black people, specifically black males, were blamed for it. When I left to head back to VMI, the mother told me I was a credit to my race. I responded with, "there are more black men like me than there are like the man who hurt her your daughter." My response stuck with Tanner's mother for quite some time.

When I got back to VMI, I was so mentally and emotionally exhausted that I needed another vacation. Tanner and I dated until just past Ring Figure, when I received a text message that he couldn't do the long-distance relationship anymore.

I picked up the phone, called him, and got his voicemail. He was supposed to come spend the weekend with me for Ring Figure but decided at the last minute he couldn't come. I would continue to try to reach out until I got a call from his new boyfriend who asked that I not call anymore.

"My Precious"

As we approached one of the most important events at VMI, Ring Figure, I had to seriously weigh my options on who I would take through the ring ceremony. Part of the ceremony was walking whomever you chose through a replica of the class ring as pictures are taken.

As a junior, Ring Figure was one of the last big traditions on the journey to completing your cadetship. Each class' ring is unique, with one side containing images that define the class, such as memorable events of the Rat-Line. The other side typically contains an arrangement of VMI images.

Though I had needed lots of help financially along the way, as I designed my ring I was determined to go through this process on my own. I politely declined offers for financial assistance.

As I spent quite some time thinking about what I was going to do, I knew my class and the Corps was not ready for two guys to walk through the ring. I had hoped that there would come a day when it wouldn't matter, but this wasn't the time. Internally, I struggled with what was fair and what was right. I knew that doing what was fair and what was right for me would potentially have disastrous effects for the class.

The question I asked myself was, would I be right? By understanding the culture and the viewpoints held by many, I knew that my actions would thrust me into the limelight and distract from everyone else. I had to decide. The struggle was swelling as I felt that the mere concern was unfair.

In the end, I couldn't bring myself to steal the attention from my class on a night that we all had worked hard to get to. Like many times before, I acknowledged the pain and moved on.

I explained to Tanner the conflict and he understood. I was able to step back and look at the forest and that little boy who had no future had made it. In the end, I took Melou Piegari through the ring. I figured it'd be fitting since her husband played a pivotal role in me getting to that point. She was the best date ever and we had a blast as we danced the night away.

A Shocking Assignment

One of the event that I was not prepared for, after I signed my contract to become an officer, was getting orders to deploy. I was not supposed to be deployed because I was in the officer training program. I was heading into my senior year and I was certain there was a mix up in the paperwork. I talked to a couple of fellow cadets and they agreed that I wasn't supposed to get orders. I decided to talk to my NCO about the issue.

During drill practices, I brought up the issue and I was told, "You're going!" I was going into my senior year. I wanted to get the opportunity to be the drum major of the regimental band and now I couldn't. I wasn't going to be able to do what I wanted to do.

My thought process and emotions were selfish at the time. After giving it some time, I thought, *how many others have paid the ultimate sacrifice? How many others had been in this situation and had to give it all up to serve our country?* I quickly resigned myself to, *you're going and you're going to make the best of the situation and VMI will all be here when I get back, if I come back.*

I called Robert and Sarah and told them I was being deployed. I told them which airport I was leaving from a week or so before my departure date. At this point, my communication with Robert and Sarah was sporadic. As the charter bus pulled up to the airport, I saw lots of families present to send their love ones off. I scanned the crowd but didn't see anyone that I recognized.

As I got off the bus, I did a second scan and realized no one was there. In all honesty, I didn't know why I expected Robert and Sarah to be there. I had figured there was a chance that I might not come back, and regardless of the broken relationship, it was a moment to mend it.

My relationship with Robert and Sarah would ebb and flow like a river throughout my time at VMI. The relationship was heavily damaged when I came out as gay. We would work on the relationship from time to time though. Sometimes they would be there and sometimes they would not. I didn't hold it against them. There were times that I felt my suspicion that I had while I lived with them in high school, of being expendable, was valid.

I felt alone. It was a moment of sadness. It was a moment I hoped no one else noticed but me. I acknowledged my feelings and kept on moving. My family were the soldiers to my left and right now as we headed off for train-ups in Indiana.

We stayed for a month or so, and as we were prepared to go into theater, I got called in and asked, "Why are you here?" I looked at the captain and the major in the room and I thought, *What are you talking about? Why am I here? You better not be saying what I think you're saying because I told y'all that before I got here.*

My mindset had changed by this point. I had accepted that I was going. I had trained with my brothers on my left and my right. I was ready to go. As we talked, I realized I was being sent back to VMI. While before I had all these emotions about not wanting to go and putting my life on hold, here I was being sent back to school and I didn't want to go back. I was angry and I wanted to stay. I wanted to do what we had been trained to do. After I was sent back to VMI, I struggled with the decision for quite some time.

<u>Truth Revealed</u>

One evening, while learning to play racquetball, I twisted my leg, injuring my knee. I didn't have insurance so I saw the on-post doctor. I didn't have the option to see a specialist or have x-rays done. The on-post doctor did what he could do for me. I just had to pray and hope that everything would heal.

During my recovery, I was away from the Army ROTC program. While I was gone, a couple of cadre members questioned cadets in reference to my sexuality and asked if they had heard me make statements in reference to being gay. I had no idea that this had happened. When I came back after being gone for a couple of months, there was a physical fitness test (PT). I took it and I failed. Because of failing the PT test, I was told that I would not be eligible to go to LDAC, the Leadership Development and Assessment Course, which was one of the prerequisites to becoming an officer in the army.

When I was told that I internalized and pointed the finger at myself. I began a slow spiral downward into depression. My career was over before it had started. What was I going to do? I asked myself. I was told that in addition to failing the PT test, I was difficult to work with and it was pointed out that I had two negligent discharges during training.

My fellow cadets found out about this and started telling me things that the cadre had said while I was gone. The despair I felt turned into anger and an urge to fight. I started realizing that I'd helped others who'd failed multiple PT tests, couldn't pass the swim test, and yet, they were still going to LDAC. It became apparent that what was being done was being done out of spite and hatred. I decided to challenge the decision.

When I went to challenge this decision, I was told I didn't have to worry about the statements that were made by the cadre in my absence. Some cadets who had struggled provided me with their testing information in order to give me a shot at being successful in the hearing. I was told all I had to worry about was my record and I was asked to just stick to the facts.

As I sat in the hearing and listened to the reasons that were given as to why I was being disqualified, I grew more and more angry. Even with being told it wasn't necessary, I had prepared myself for this hearing.

I spoke up, I spoke out, and I spoke loudly. I stated, "This is not about failing a PT test. What is happening to me right now is because some of the cadre suspect that I'm gay and they don't want homosexuals or gay people in the military." To make a statement like that in a hearing jarred and surprised many people who were in the room.

The response to that was that I had better have proof to make such a statement. I started to read the following letters from fellow cadets:

Letter 1

A cadetship spanning four years can tell you a lot about a brother rat. As a member of the same Company and ROTC as Deuntay Diggs. I can fully say that I know him well as a person and as a cadet. This young man has, in my opinion, conquered adversity and come out as a confident, trusting, and genuine person. I see someone who has been under ridicule from peers and superiors, but has learned from the challenges presented to him. Through it all he has continued to follow his heart and stay true to himself. Deuntay Diggs represents an honest and reliable person, unafraid to speak up for what he believes in and ready to take on new challenges. I undoubtedly believe he has the incentive and poise to lead others, and the willingness to learn from those around him. He is a brother rat that I trust and a man that I would be proud to serve next to.

Cadet C.B.Z.

Letter 2

On Behalf of Cadet Diggs
May 3, 2007 (1616 Hours)
To Whom It May Concern:

     I was asked by Cadet Diggs to write a statement on his behalf to keep him in the VMI AROTC program. I know Diggs is planning to graduate in December of 2007 after he completes BOLC I/Warrior Forge. I am writing to defend Cadet Diggs because I'm told the "powers that be" think he does not work well with others.

     I met Diggs during my MS one year but I really got to know him during the summer of 2005 while we were both attending OSUT at Fort Benning, Georgia. During my time there I came across Diggs multiple times. He always acted in a professional manner and worked well with his training platoon. Even when he was not in a leadership role, (he was a platoon guide for a time) privates continued to come to him for guidance for various reasons. I have personally worked with him at our home unit here in Lexington B/1/116th VARNG and in the two years we have been there, he has contributed as much as any other cadet. In addition, to my knowledge, he has never received any reprimands and the only problems I have heard of were when the unit fouled up paper work when trying to mobilize for the deployment to Kosovo. He always remains respectful and the problem was solved with little incident. Now that he is back with us as a cadet, our commander has expected the same from him as the rest of the cadets; and to my knowledge he has delivered. In regards to him supposedly having trouble working with others, I have never seen anything that would lead me to believe that is true. In fact it was cadet Diggs, during an MS three lab this semester that look after an MS one that had arrived late from SVU. Diggs took it upon himself to help this kid find where he was going. In lab, while not the most "ra ra ra...energetic" person out, his commitment to the team he is assigned and his competence is better then some of the scholarship kids the army thinks are worthy of wasting money on.

In short, I have never had a problem working with Cadet Diggs and would prefer him over some of the other people that I have been assigned by the Army department, because while Diggs may not be what the AROTC thinks a cadet should be, he is always out there. At the very least he is looking after people, and is that not what a cadet and an officer is supposed to do...look after the people under him?

Respectfully submitted
Cadet S., J.S.
MS 3 (VMI Class 2008)

Letter 3

May 7, 2007

To Whom It May Concern,

Cadet Diggs has requested that I write a letter addressing what I have observed of his character and attitude when participating in VMI AROTC training activities with him. In the time that I have been at VMI, I have known him to be a competent and caring individual with a dedication to his friends, school and country that is unmatched. I have never seen him turn someone down when asking for help, nor single anyone out for any type of difference or shortcoming. During much of our training, he has offered to carry extra loads, and take on more demanding jobs when others are struggling. His performance as a team player is unmatched. He does not flee from adversity. He has never let me or anyone I know down when they have asked something of him. I have never seen him put anything but the best forward when he is presented with a challenge. Cadet Diggs is one of the few people I meet who harbor no hatred or prejudice towards anything or anyone. I am proud to have trained and worked with Deuntay as a VMI AROTC cadet, and look forward to working with him again as an officer.

Very Respectfully,

S.B.

Letter 4

K., M.K.

Personal Statement

Recently I have been informed by Cadet Diggs that he is being removed from the VMI AROTC program. He told me that this has been in the works for awhile, but came to a close after he failed the most recent APFT. I know that the failure of one APFT cannot be reason enough to disenroll a cadet because there have been cadets whose physical abilities were far more lacking than Cadet Diggs' that have received gold bars from this wonderful program. Cadet Diggs informed me that a major reason for the cancellation of his contract was the alleged fact that he does not work well with others. I know that this fact is alleged because I am an 'other' who has never had a problem working with Cadet Diggs. I also know of many 'others' who are of the same opinion. I went to army basic training and Ft. Benning's School of Infantry with Cadet Diggs. In my short 20 years of life I have never run across so many disagreeable 'others' than during my summer at beautiful Ft. Benning. I know for a fact that Cadet Diggs was well liked and far exceeded the standards during our 14 weeks of training. This is admirable because there were plenty of privates there who could not even say they liked themselves, much less anyone else.

So, the alleged fact that Cadet Diggs does not work well with others, in my opinion, has as much validity as the statement, "The sky is green." It's definitely possible, but I've never seen it. While it is true that there are those who do not like Cadet Diggs, I think it is equally true that even members of that opinion group would disagree with the decision made by the VMI AROTC department. I personally think that Cadet Diggs would make an excellent officer and that his troubles mainly lie within the interesting and paradoxical environment of AROTC land. I cannot say for sure, but it seems reasonable to me that there are officers in the army that are not well liked, and still have the ability to get the job done. I can see how the heavily weighted opinions of the close minded and prejudiced few could conjure up this opinion of Cadet Diggs. However, as someone who has actually had to work with Cadet Diggs, I can say with confidence that I wholeheartedly disagree.

Respectfully,

Cadet K, M.K.
VMI AROTC MSIII

As I read each letter, the shock on some of the faces of those in attendance was priceless. I concluded reading the letters. The hearing was stopped and I was sent on to LDAC. I had won the battle.

Up to that point, no matter what people said or did, I had never really fought that hard, caused a scene or went to the papers. I'd gotten in one fight after being picked on in Cocke Hall. It was never about garnering attention. For me, it was about helping people grow, doing the right thing, them challenging me, and helping me grow as well. I felt vindicated. I felt powerful and strong.

Travel Abroad

Shortly after the previous situation had occurred, I learned that I had earned a scholarship to study abroad in Morocco for the summer. Dr. Taifi, and his wife, Khadijah, were both excellent teachers. They were patient and taught Arabic in a way that captivated and intrigued me. I was shocked that I had gotten the opportunity to visit Morocco. This would be my first time outside of the country.

I eagerly went through the process to get the appropriate paperwork taken care of and to get my passport. As the day arrived to board the plane to Morocco, I was bursting with energy and couldn't wait to be immersed in the culture and language.

As I touched down in Morocco, and we were all gathered at the entrance to the airport, Dr. Taifi gave us all instructions on what was going to happen and a few of the dos and don'ts.

Out of all the things I was told, I paid close attention to the warning to not take photos of the police and the military. As I looked around, I felt a bit of anxiety at the fact that I was no longer in the United States.

After I got my luggage, the group of students and I were escorted to a white van. Once in the van, we headed towards the Arabic Language Institute of Fez (ALIF). After we drove for about an hour, one of the passengers noticed a police car was coming up behind us at a fast pace with the lights activated.

We all turned around, confused about what was happening. We were in the middle of nowhere. I couldn't for the life of me figure out where they came from. I had guessed the driver must have been speeding. The driver pulled over, and the patrol car pulled up behind us.

Two police officers exited their patrol vehicle and approached on both sides. One spoke with the driver while the other spoke with Dr. Taifi.

After a brief conversation, Dr. Taifi turned to us and assured us everything was okay. He explained that we needed to get out. I looked at him and thought, *get out of what?* My mind was racing, and I thought, *we 'bout to die.* We had been in the country for just a few hours, and this had already happened.

As we got out of the van and lined up, I tried to figure out my escape route. Truth be told, I wasn't going to make it far because it was just open land. I was going to try, though. One of the police officers walked over to a female that was attached to our group from NY and asked for her camera. I looked at her like and thought, *you better not have done what I think you did.*

The female said, "There are no pictures of you." She began to show the police officer the pictures on the camera to confirm. *Oh, sweet baby Jesus!* I said to myself. I saw Heaven and Hell in that moment. Typically, I'm slow to anger, but in that moment, I went from 0 to 100 quickly. I thought to myself, *I don't mess with the police in my country. What makes you think I want to play around in a foreign country?*

After it was confirmed that there were no pictures taken, we were given a stern warning and allowed back on the van to carry on. Once we got back in the van, everyone was upset with the female who had gotten us into the predicament. I looked at her and said, "We ain't in Kansas anymore Dorothy! Don't you ever do that again!"

She responded with, "I didn't actually take the picture. I was just looking through the camera."

I said, "Well, look through your eyes and put that thing away."

She said, "Well, I don't understand what the problem is," as she looked around the van for support. As I rolled my eyes, I said, "Girl, you don't have to understand. Just do as you're told."

Once we got to ALIF, we were fed one of the best meals I had ever tasted, Moroccan couscous with a side of Moroccan tea. After our meal, we were given a tour, and then it was time to split up.

Some went with their respective host families, and a few of us stayed on campus. I decided to stay on campus because staying with a host family meant that I wouldn't have had the amenities I was accustomed to. When I found out that I had to use a squat toilet, I thought to myself, *ohh no, not me.*

When I was at infantry school, I refused to dig a hole and have a bowel movement. I just held it in. My drill sergeants were shocked when they had learned that I went an entire week without having a bowel movement in a hole. For, me the fear of having a bowel movement on my own ankles or legs was something I wasn't willing to entertain.

Some people have a negative view point about what being Muslim or being an Arab is. It is not until you go and experience these cultures that you find that certain things people say are not representative of the entire religion or people.

Overall, I found the people of Morocco to be beautiful, generous, and kind-hearted. While studying in Morocco, I grew my hair out. I was comfortable enough with the language to travel solo at times. I would go to hotels that had nightclubs and dance the night away.

Dancing for me is a time you can be free and shut out the stresses of the world. I didn't need alcohol or drugs. I just needed good music, and I'd dance all night long. It would frustrate me when I would be offered drugs.

As I brushed off the person who offered the drugs to me, in my head I thought, *do I look like I do drugs?* Looking back, I probably did. At this point, it had happened multiple times in the states, as well as now in a foreign country. I guess people aren't used to seeing someone on a natural high enjoying themselves, not caring who's watching.

Prior to going to Morocco, I had looked at travel sites for information on LGBT safety. Most sites warned that conducting a homosexual act could be punishable with up to three years imprisonment. I also read that LGBT people traveling to Morocco should use discretion but would find that there is a gay culture.

As I started to become acclimated to the country, I was initially confused. I saw men holding hands, and I quickly learned that this was a sign of friendship and didn't mean anything more. I was determined to find the underground gay scene, but it was a risky adventure. I couldn't do anything that would bring shame to VMI. I was not going to prison. While there was a desire to find the gay scenes, it wasn't my primary reason for being in the country.

My first friendship with a native Moroccan was a young barber named Anis who owned his own shop. He was in his early twenties, fit, and he spoke broken English. As I stumbled upon his shop, I decided to venture in to get an edge up.

There were two barbers, and the set-up was very similar to what I was used to. It had a row of seats on the left for waiting customers and two barber chairs on the right. As we spoke, I revealed that I was in Fez on a study abroad trip, and that I was from America.

Anis was very excited to learn about America and wanted to hear what I thought about Morocco. As he finished the edge up he said, "You stay and we have tea." You didn't have to ask me twice! I loved the taste of Moroccan tea. I found myself a little conflicted because an attractive man had asked me to stay for tea, but I reminded myself that the culture is different than what I was accustomed to.

As we shared tea and talked, time flew by. Before I knew it, it was late. At this time, Anis offered me dinner and the option of staying the night. Now call me crazy but I said, "Why not? I'll stay." I was trying to figure out where exactly I had agreed to stay. Surely, we weren't having dinner in the barber shop, and we weren't going to sleep there.

Anis hugged his employee and bid him farewell. After the employee walked out of the shop door, he locked it. He then walked back towards me, and as he walked past me, he eagerly said, "Come."

We walked to the back of the shop to a curtain. As he slid the curtain to the side, stairs were revealed. Up the stairs we went, and in my head, I thought, *what did I just get myself into?* As we reached the top of the stairs, I saw that Anis had a sparsely furnished studio apartment.

There were no tables and no furniture in his studio apartment. He told me to come sit as he motioned to a carpet that was in the center of the room. As I sat there, he walked over to the corner of the room and grabbed a towel that he laid down in front of me. He then went over to the kitchen area and began preparing food.

I closely watched, because I wasn't sure exactly what he was preparing. I was nervous because I didn't want to be rude, but I knew if it didn't appear right or smell right, I wasn't going to eat it. As he prepared dinner, the topics of conversation continuously changed. Most of the time was spent correcting my pronunciation of words.

Finally, dinner was served, and it was a traditional Moroccan dish called Tagine. I cautiously took a piece of bread and dipped it into the stew. I noticed that he was anxiously waiting for a response on how the meal tasted. I tried not to make any faces as I chewed. I looked down and said in a quiet voice مذاق سيء (bad taste). Anis leaned forward with a look of concern. I smiled, and said "just joking. It's really good." It took a few seconds for him to understand I was joking but we had an awesome meal together.

As the night rolled on, eventually it came time for bed. As I looked around, it became abundantly clear that we were going to be sleeping on the floor. This didn't bother me because I had grown up doing this. I had also slept on the ground during field training.

Anis grabbed a couple of blankets and placed them on the floor. I looked at the blankets and thought to myself, *they are awfully close.* When I saw the pillow, I thought, *ohh naww. I just met you, I'm not sharing a pillow.* Petty, I know. I had already shared a meal and said I would stay.

He laid down in his full clothes and I beside him. I thought to myself, *this has got to be the strangest but most enjoyable time I've ever had.* Anis fell fast asleep, but I could not. I spent the night staring at the ceiling. The next morning, I got up and rushed back to campus where I showered, brushed my teeth, and rushed into class.

As I told everyone about my experience, my classmates were shocked and called me crazy. Of course, I got asked whether Anis was gay. I replied, "I don't know, and it really doesn't matter. I have a new friend to explore the city with. Before any of you judge me, some of you spent the night in a random stranger's home as well." Most laughed and replied with, "You have a point."

As time went on, Anis and I became very close, and true to his word, he took me all over Fez. It got to the point where I would spend the night and wake up to Anis with an arm and foot over me. At this point, some of my male classmates were sure he was gay. When the topic would be discussed, I would reply with, "I'd rather have a solid friend than test the waters and mess things up." The guys would smile and say, "Uhm okay. Whatever."

One day after class, Anis showed up at ALIF, and he asked if I wanted to invite a friend along to explore the city. I said, "Sure!" I invited one of the females in the group to come along. We went through our normal routine, and at the end of the night, we all three ended up sharing the floor. I was so mad because she was now between us. I had to check myself. Had I started to gain feelings for Anis?

The next day, back in class, I made it clear to the female not to say anything about me being gay and that I hadn't told Anis. She understood. At the end of class, Anis arrived again, but this time, he wanted to just go with the female. He said she was very beautiful, and he wanted to take her to dinner.

I tried to hide the frustration and mentioned how I thought it was an awesome idea especially since I had to listen all day to her talk about how sexy Anis was. I watched as they walked off together. I was so mad, but there was nothing to be done. As quickly as our friendship began, it ended, and their relationship grew.

On Excursion

One of the things I wanted to do while I was in Morocco was travel to Gibraltar, which is a British territory. After being in the country for a while, I got the opportunity to make the trip. I took a train with a couple of classmates across Morocco and then took a ferry to get there.

While I visited, I spent time at Catalan Bay where I met a British officer in the Royal Navy. As we chatted over a brief period of time, I was eventually offered an opportunity to be snuck on base to hang out. I gladly accepted.

As I got lost in the experience, I forgot about the time, and I ended up missing the ferry back to Morocco. Panic-stricken, I realized that I was now alone with very little money. There was one ferry left, and so I waited for the last trip, and the British Officer waited with me.

Once on the ferry, I felt a little bit of relief because I knew I was one step closer to getting back to Fez. I knew missing class the next morning wasn't an option. As we docked, and I got off the Ferry, I saw the hustle and bustle and started to panic even more. I began wondering where I should start. Would I have enough money to make it back?

While I figured out a game plan, I overheard three women who spoke English talking about finding a way to get back to Fez. I couldn't believe it. I interrupted them and asked if they were from America. When one of them replied, "Yes." I told them I was too.

As we tried to figure out how we were getting back, we learned that all the trains and buses had left for the night. The only option was a taxi, which would be expensive due to our destination being approximately three hours away. We frantically searched and found a taxi driver who would be willing to take us. I think in that moment they were more comfortable because they had me, and I was more comfortable because I had them.

As we struck out on our way to Fez, I sat in the front seat and the ladies sat in the backseat. Along the journey, the taxi driver stopped at the gas station to get gas. I thought, *they're about to take us all*. I don't know who *"they"* even were. I was primed by what I had seen on television. I thought, *they're going to take these ladies, and they're going to kill me. We're going to be sold or something. They're going to kidnap us.* We looked at each other and we knew that each of us was thinking the same thing.

The taxi driver disappeared inside of the store for what seemed like forever and then reappeared. As he walked out of the gas station, all four of us stared at him. He walked around the back of the car, grabbed the nozzle and pumped the gas.

In the end, the driver was professional, and we made it safely back to Fez. I wish I knew how those ladies are doing now and how life has treated them.

I showed up one hour before class started. I told everyone about my wild adventure. Everyone again told me I was crazy. It was an adventure of a lifetime. I successfully completed my Arabic courses early and prepared to board the plane to travel to the State of Washington for the Leader Development and Assessment Course (LDAC). I was nervous when I arrived in Morocco, and I was sad when I had to leave Morocco early. From the city to the countryside I found Morocco to be a beautiful country.

On the plane back to the states, I knew that the fun was over, and it was now time to focus, for I had to prove to all who had doubted my ability to successfully complete LDAC, that they were wrong. LDAC was held at Fort Lewis. I found it to be challenging yet familiar.

Everything that I had done through VMI and infantry school prepared me for all the tests. The only test that I hesitated on was the Combat Water Survival Test. In order to successfully complete this challenge, I had to complete ten minutes of constant swimming, five minutes of treading water, an underwater gear ditch, distance gear swim, and finally a ten-meter blindfolded jump with a rifle.

As I climbed the steps of the diving board, fear began to set in with each step. Once on the diving board, I looked at the instructor, and he could see the fear in my eyes. The instructor looked at me and whispered, "You got this." He then told me to pull the toboggan cap down and to hold my rifle with both hands out in front of me and step off. He repeated his instructions a second time, and as I pulled the cap down everything went dark. "Now step off," the instructor said again in a hushed tone. "You got this."

I stood there for what felt like an eternity. Then I stepped. As my body hit the water, I knew at that moment there was nothing left standing between me and my commission. All the hard work, patience, and support had paid off.

I went on to pass all requirements needed to earn my commission. Initially, I couldn't wait to get back to VMI and brag and boast about what I had done, but those emotions were fleeting. I remained excited on the inside but maintained my composure. I let my success be my voice.

Back at the Institute

In my senior year I become a Dyke, which is a senior mentor. Every senior has a Rat, which is a freshman that they coach and mentor, teaching them how to get through VMI. You help them to successfully navigate without being boned (getting in trouble), receiving demerits, or marching PT's (penalty tours). You help them learn to balance the three-legged stool. When I became a Dyke, I wanted to do things a bit differently.

When you're a Rat you don't have a choice. You must take whichever mentor picks you. I allowed my Rats to choose me, which was unheard of at the time. Having me as their Dyke was going to be different, though. It was going to be something new, due to me being gay. I didn't want to ruin their VMI experience.

As the ratline kicked off, I became known as a "Rat-Daddy." Though I believed in the system of VMI, I felt like there were enough people that were tough and strict on the Rats. I was the counter balance to that. I tried to mentor and pass on everything that I had learned so that everyone I encountered would be successful.

I had learned throughout my cadetship that, if there was a cadet who was suicidal or a cadet who was dealing with significant trauma, I was able to use my life experiences to help them. I learned that being ashamed and keeping things bottled up only made things worse. I drew on that knowledge, and it made me an even better Dyke.

I was constantly putting currency into the bank of trust. No matter what happened at VMI, whenever there was an opportunity for me to go public when something wrong was said or done, I didn't. I believed in the system at VMI, and I felt like it was my job to protect it, just like everyone else. The system may not have been perfect, but it was as close as it got.

Now in my senior year, having made it through most of the storms, my goal was to be the best Dyke that I could be for both of my Rats, Chris and Eddie. As Rats, neither could have cell phones in their rooms, so I kept their phones in my room. The main priority was to make sure they contacted their parents and kept them informed.

For some parents, it is difficult to send their children off to VMI because to them, it's this wild place with a strange language, strict rules, and mean upperclassmen. I wanted to ensure that both of my Rats' parents knew that they were okay.

As the Rat-Line continued, I don't recall ever raising my voice at my Rats. I didn't need to. They did what I asked of them, and they were way better academically than I was. As my Rats navigated the Rat-Line, I was so proud to watch them grow into fourth classmen. Whenever either would falter, I was always right there to help them. I asked for nothing in return. I truly just wanted both men to be successful and happy. In my head, I chuckle at the last sentence. I can visualize a third-classmen, currently in attendance at VMI, reading the last sentence; thinking, "what a load of cow puck; no Rat is supposed to be happy."

In the moments of mentoring and looking after my Rats, doing what I believed was right, not for personal gain, but because it was the right thing to do, I was building a foundation for life after VMI. I was setting the stage for my life in Fredericksburg, VA long before I even knew it existed or that I would move there. Trusting in the process, and following the cardinal rule--treat others as you want to be treated--were going to be the recipes for opportunities and blessings that I couldn't have even imaged.

Regimental Band

Throughout my entire time at VMI, I was in the regimental band under the direction of Colonel Brodie. He was full of energy and full of life. He was very down-to-earth with a common-sense approach to life. I couldn't say enough about him. He understood VMI and had been there for quite some time. Colonel Brodie just got it, and not just from a faculty perspective, but also from a cadet's approach and mindset as well.

He was the person that understood the importance and significance of what we did but also understood that there was a time and a place where you could have a little bit of fun and relax. He was always important to me because any time that I needed a laugh and life was too much, he was there.

Colonel Brodie had the unique ability to keep things light even when it was a serious matter. Under his direction, I performed with the Regimental Band and Glee Club (which is singing). I also participated in jazz band, but I wasn't as interested in that.

I wanted to be a part of anything he was involved with. I looked up to and respected him so much for who he is, the direction he gave and his outlook on life. In my efforts to be a good Dyke, I attempted to emulate Colonel Brodie, often times, asking myself, *what would Colonel Brodie do?*

Finish Line

During my last summer at VMI, I lived off post for summer school. I lived with a couple of Brother-Rats. It was a new experience moving into an apartment and living with roommates. I had lived my entire cadetship with other people, but it was different when I had to pay money and figure things out. Learning to live on my own and not having to answer to anybody felt great. I quickly learned how to manage money.

Due to my lack of academic success, I had to stay a fifth-year at VMI. I had to give the dean at the time, Brigadier General Brower, so much credit. He looked at my situation of struggling academically, and acknowledged the work that I put in to turn the situation around and become successful. As a fifth-year cadet, I felt like an emperor. Nobody messed with fifth-year cadets. For instance, if you didn't want to march in the parade, you didn't have to march in the parade. Being in the regimental band, I loved parades, so I marched. You kind of did what you wanted as a fifth-year cadet. It was interesting because you were still a part of the VMI system, which is very regimented, but at the same time, you're not.

The Cycle is Broken

I successfully graduated in December 2007. After graduation, I took time to reflect on my life and how far I had come. I couldn't help but think of all my accomplishments—it felt surreal, as if I needed to be pinched to be woken from a dream. I looked around at all my support.

I commissioned as an officer in the Army Reserves. My first salute was to Sergeant Major Neel of the corps of cadets. Just having him there and having earned his respect meant the world to me. All the people who had followed my cadetship, and who had either helped me around some of the potholes or helped lift me out of the potholes, were there to support me.

It was an amazing moment in time. As I walked across the stage, I knew that there was nothing that this world could throw at me that I could not handle. One of the things that immediately struck me in that moment was that I did not get there by myself. I did the brunt of the work, and I took the brunt of the punishment, but every step of the way, there were people placed by God in my path to guide me.

While I would love to say that I was able to recover academically and end with a high GPA, that wasn't the case. I finished college with a 2.0. While I had anomalous life events during my cadetship that contributed to my GPA being low, I would tell anyone struggling to ask for help early and not let pride or ego become an obstacle to success.

After I graduated, I was ready to take on the world. I had secured my first job, and I had gotten lost in the title of executive. I thought there was going to be smooth sailing ahead, but life dealt some major curve balls. Little did I know, but the stage was being set for me to go down an unintended path. It was a path that would result in me gaining a platform and reaching over 90 million people across the world.

About the Author

Deuntay Diggs is a law enforcement officer, mentor, motivational speaker, host of "Cooking With Love Show" on Facebook Live, singer, viral dancing star, and now a self-published author. He resides in Fredericksburg, VA with his husband, Benjamin Diggs.

Connect with Deuntay on his website at **www.deuntaydiggs.com**. You never know what adventure he will be on next. He strives to make a difference and push others to live their best life.

82330841R00095

Made in the USA
San Bernardino, CA
16 July 2018